William J. Richardson, S. J.

Reflections
in memoriam

edited by
Babette Babich

51ˢᵗ meeting of the
Heidegger Circle
30 March – 2 April 2017

Julia Ireland, Convenor

Whitman College, Walla Walla, Washington
NNS Press
New York City, NY

For Bill's family,
for Bill's friends,
&
for his students,

including future students
of Heidegger's thought
& Lacanian psychoanalysis

CONTENTS

PREFACE v
LEO O'DONOVAN 1
RICHARD KEARNEY 8
DANIEL DAHLSTROM 14
PINA MONETA 16
ROBERT INNIS 20
RICHARD BOOTHBY 21
JEFFREY BLOECHL 22
SCOTT M. CAMPBELL 24
DIETER BRUMM 27
BABETTE BABICH 29
GRAEME NICHOLSON 36
RICHARD CAPOBIANCO 38
JEAN GRONDIN 39
PAUL BRUNO, ED McGUSHIN, AND SCOTT CAMPBELL ... 42
THOMAS SHEEHAN 44
GENE PALUMBO 54
PETER LUPARIO 56
ON HEIDEGGER TO LACAN 64
WILLIAM J. RICHARDSON, S.J., BIBLIOGRAPHY 97

PREFACE

Fr. William J. Richardson, S.J., was born in Brooklyn, New York on the 2nd of November, 1920. He died at the Jesuit Campion Health Center, in Weston, Massachusetts, on the 10th of December, 2016.

Leo O'Donovan, S.J., Richard Kearney, and Jeffrey Bloechl, each in different ways gathered the diffusions of mourning friends, students, colleagues, patients, and admirers of the late William J. Richardson, via email over the days leading up to and after his funeral. Bill was one of the founding members of the Heidegger Circle (Penn State, 1967) and was present at the first conference on Heidegger's thought held in 1964.

Julia Ireland, convenor of the 51st meeting of the Heidegger Circle, 2017, at Whitman College in the state of Washington, asked me if I might take up the task of gathering a few words and recollections in his memory for the sake of the members of the Circle.

I offer this volume in response to that request, drawn from direct responses and email recollections. Here is a first pass at such reflections, *in memoriam*.

Babette Babich
New York City
24 March 2017

REFLECTIONS

LEO O'DONOVAN

MAKING SENSE
In Memory of
William J. Richardson, S.J.
(2 November 1920–10 December 2016)[1]

In my last extended conversation with Bill, I asked him whether he was in any pain and he told me that he was not. "Few people at 96 are cared for as well as I am, Leo," he added. What was he thinking about? I asked. And he said that he was "spending his time trying to make sense of these last days."

And that was, in many ways, what he had been doing all his life. Making sense of things through a life at the center of which was his giving his word and keeping it.

His faith was fierce, wrested from the absurdity of life and won, through grace, again and again — for us first, his family and students. For aren't all of us here really his students, following him into the time of making sense not just of this world and our lives in it but, well, yes, Being, the real from which all realities arise. Seeking sense and finding the

---

[1] Homily for Bill Richardson's funeral mass. Campion Centre, Weston, MA, 14 Dec 2016.

word to express it, was that not his life? And was there anyone for whom the word of meaning he sought was more clearly not an answer but a mystery, not a problem to be solved but a fullness of meaning beyond all human expression?

Shall we call that mystery God? It's a staggering claim. Who can make it? St. Paul, certainly. Who can separate us, he wrote to the Romans, from the love of Christ? What earthly sorrow or calamity, what overwhelming loss of meaning?

"If God is for us, who is against us? He who did not spare his own Son but gave him up for us all, will he not also give us all things with him?" wrote Paul. All things! "Who shall separate us from the love of Christ? Shall tribulation, or distress, or persecution, or famine, or nakedness, or peril, or sword?"

"No, in all these things we are more than conquerors through him who loved us. For I am sure that neither death, nor life, nor angels, nor principalities, nor things present, nor things to come, nor powers, nor height, nor depth, nor anything else in all creation, will be able to separate us from the love of God in Christ Jesus our Lord." (Rom 8.31-39)

Bill's search for meaning was a faith because it took its ground and dynamic not from a philosophical conviction of the reality of God, a conventional theism, if you will, but from an embodied, an incarnate word, a word made flesh, with all the frailty, the absurdity and the risk that entails. The word of Bill's life, the word he made and gave was called forth and rooted in the Word given us in Jesus, the revelation through Jesus that we are born not by some natural accident but *for* an enveloping love.

Don't make it too easy here, Leo, he might well say now. Don't be sentimental. He once told me of an unhelpful retreat he had made where he felt he could have dandled the retreat master like a child in his lap. And surely at this moment, for this man, I shudder to think I might speak without being serious (in the French sense).

No, the word, of his life and of his and our savior, is not easy, obvious, something readily at hand. It is not heard in a whirlwind, or felt in an earthquake, nor in a blazing fire. It is heard, if one listens intently, in "a still small voice or whisper" that conveys the promise of the Holy Mystery before whom, as with Elijah, we cover our faces and stand waiting. (I Kings 19.11-16) It is truth that unveils itself, whether we will it or not, and unveils *us* at the same time, or better said, unveils and reveals us to ourselves through the future, an absolute future, which calls forth our time.

We do not master or easily make sense of this word of truth. Rather, it masters us and makes sense of us. It calls us not to certainty but to trust, trust in small increments, like a scientist's experiments to realize the scientist's hypothesis, or an artist's campaign to fulfill the artist's vision. To believe in the midst of such searching required for Bill a surrender of the securities of easy confidence. It manifested itself in the genuineness, the authenticity, the integrity that made his classes and lectures events of revelation. To prepare something worthy of his students or visitors to a lecture was an agonizing ordeal for him, carried often into the early morning of the presentation — and always accompanied by a literary or historical event that would connect the presentation with what William James called the cash value of the matter or, as Bill would put it: "So what?"

He was clearly brilliant. Light shone from him as from a diamond. But he needed the mirror of his friends and students to see his own light. How often did Bill ask one or another of us for advice on a simple practical matter — about a car to drive, a jacket to wear, a meal to serve? And yet there always recurred, because it could not be planned or controlled, the deep-throated laughter, the joy of sharing something beautiful, the catharsis of great drama. (What was your favorite play or movie seen with Bill? I have no count of them, but know that they ranged from "A Funny Thing Happened on the Way to the Forum" to "Long Day's Journey into Night.")

Giving your word while trying to make sense of things is costly. You might have given it in a way you think you now cannot bear. You may have let it take you in a direction you now regret. But it must be given, if you are to make any sense of life rather than accept a final darkness as our fate. *Credo ut intelligam*, wrote Anselm. I believe in order to understand. Or, to quote a more contemporary voice: Dag Hammarskjold wrote on Whitsunday 1961:

> I don't know Who — or what — put the question, I don't know when it was put. I don't even remember answering. But at some moment I did answer *Yes* to Someone — or Something — and from that hour I was certain that existence is meaningful and that, therefore, my life, in self-surrender, had a goal.
>
> From that moment I have known what it means "not to look back," and "to take no thought for the morrow."

Hammarskjold's reflection went further.

> Led by the Ariadne's thread of my answer through the labyrinth of Life, I

came to a time and place where I realized that the Way leads to a triumph which is a catastrophe, and to a catastrophe which is a triumph, that the price for committing one's life would be reproach, and the only elevation possible to man lies in the depths of humiliation. After that, the word "courage" lost its meaning, since nothing could be taken from me.

As I continued along the Way, I learned, step by step, word by word, that behind every saying in the Gospels stands *one* man and *one* man's experience. Also behind the prayer that the cup might pass from him and his promise to drink it. Also behind each of the words from the Cross.

Some years ago I learned from Bill the story of how Martin Heidegger, anticipating his death and memorial service, asked his former student Fr. Bernhard Welte, S.J., to speak for him. But how should I do that, Professor Heidegger, Welte replied, since you have not understood yourself as a believer. Take the text from Luke, said Heidegger: "Ask and you shall receive; seek and you shall find; knock and it will be opened to you." (Lk 11.9-10) "Speak about that."

Ask and you shall receive; seek and you shall find; knock and it will be opened to you. Struggle to pose the question; stress its search, force it forward. Set off on the journey. When tempted to turn back, set off again. Ask, seek, knock.

Bill *asked* at the College of the Holy Cross, in tights playing "Richard II" or in debates partnered with Edward Bennett Williams. He *sought* in all but heroic doctoral studies and the pursuit of the Maître-Agrégé at Louvain. He *knocked* at the introduction to thought for students at St. Peter's College and a Jesuit Scholasticate in New York, and then for 17 years at Fordham University and on for more than three decades at Boston College.

He *asked* for the sense of his experience and ours at whatever cost, often to his own surrender of comfort or ease — or sleep. He *sought* even when the search was into darkness that he could describe with frightening acuity. He *knocked* even at the door of the meaningless. Yet ever and again he spoke the word of his life, his Yes to the God of his existence and ours, his commitment as assured as the dawn, as multi-hued as the sunset.

And now, as we hope and pray, our hearts taken away with him, he is receiving, and finding, and it is being opened to him.

This is, is it not? our hope. His final giving of himself into the light that makes sense of all, the light that he questioned and sought and probed, as much as Jacob with the angel, until now he can give us his last and most precious gift: a vision of that light into which he has entered, oh, through what can only be called grace, in utter peace.

Peacefully. Peacefully. Peacefully.

> **Readings**:
> 1 Kings 19:9-13
> Romans 8:31-39
> Luke 11:1-4, 9-10

Leo J. O'Donovan, S.J.
President *emeritus*
Georgetown University

RICHARD KEARNEY

Bill was a beautiful man. [2]

He was a wise deep elegant curious brilliant scrupulous angry chivalrous tormented honest kind stubborn inspiring funny loving beautiful man.

I first met Bill at my doctoral dissertation in Paris in June 1980. He came to hear the philosopher, Emmanuel Levinas, who was a member of my examining committee as he had been for Bill's classic dissertation on Heidegger in Leuven some

---

[2] Reminiscence at Bill Richardson's wake – Campion Centre, Weston, MA, Dec 13, 2016.

twenty years previously. After the exam, Bill approached me and invited me to come to Boston College. I did and I am still here.

During the thirty six years of our acquaintance, Bill became not only a great friend, confidant and colleague but also a regular visitor to our house in Boston for festive dinners with students as well as Thanksgiving and Easter Sunday with the family. He was very close to my wife, Anne, and our two daughters, Simone and Sarah, who referred to him as their 'American granddad'. (They referred to his adorable sister, Peg, whom we stayed with regularly in NYC, as their 'American Grandma'). The girls, growing up, were enthralled by his annual Thanksgiving recitations by the fireside — after some 'strong tea' imbibed from a special Waterford Glass Peg gave us — when he would rise to his feet, legs akimbo, hands on hips, head high, and recite a favorite rousing speech from *Hamlet, Henry IV* or *Richard III* (whom he had originally played as a young student at Holy Cross College in 1940. Bill was a devoted thespian to the end).

I have many stories of Bill during our times in Paris, Boston and at annual SPEP conferences. But I will limit myself here to just one which occurred in his father's native Ireland.

It was in July 1996 when Bill, staying with us in Dublin, asked if we might drive him north to visit his father's homestead. Bill's father was a Protestant who wore the Ulster Orange Sash on Loyalist holidays in protest against Irish papists! Bill, brought up Catholic by his mother, waited until his father died before joining the Jesuits. As Bill and I drove north, accompanied by my wife Anne and our ten year old daughter Sarah, all he knew (from childhood memory) was that his father's farm was called 'Grovewill' and was located somewhere in the townland of Dungannon in Country Tyrone. It was still during the Troubles in Northern Ireland and we had to pass through army checkpoints at the Border to get there.

Arriving in Dungannon, we went to the Post Office to inquire where the old Richardson farm was, but no one knew. We then asked at the local grocers, butchers, public house, parsonage, but were repeatedly met with blank stares. No one knew of Grovehill farm. About to depart, tails between our legs, Bill suggested we have one last try. He pointed to the local army outpost — all concrete walls and barbed wire — and proceeded to walk inside with Anne.

Twenty minutes later, out they came accompanied by an army police van. Apparently when Bill had mentioned Grovehill farm, the officer on duty recognized it as a place that had been firebombed by the IRA the previous night! So off we set with an army escort through rolling hills and drumlins until we reached Bill's father's homestead.

We were greeted at the door by an affable farmer who welcomed Bill like a long lost brother. 'Come in! come in! Old Charlie Richardson sold us this farm and any Richardson is welcome home!' Charlie was Bill's uncle who had inherited the farm when Bill's father (Frederick) emigrated to New York, meeting Bill's mother (Margaret Oliver) while he was waiting at table on a transatlantic liner. She was returning from a European Grand Tour.

We were invited into the firebombed kitchen and sat by the hearth where the farmer served Bill a jar of 'strong tea' (native Bushmills) and regaled us with tales of his families' heroic resistance to IRA campaigns of aggression. Meanwhile our small daughter Sarah, who had wandered upstairs to the bathroom, returned to whisper in my ear that there were 'photos of men wearing orange uniforms upstairs'. I realised right away that we were sitting in a bastion of Orange Ulster Protestantism! At this moment, our host nudged Bill on the elbow and pointed to the main entrance.

'Do you see that threshold Bill?'

Bill nodded.

'In four hundred years not one Papist has passed that door! They tried to drive us out with bullet and bomb, with terror and taunt, but we would not go. No surrender!'. At which point, he turns to Bill and asks, 'And what do you do yourself, Bill?'

Bill stared down into his 'strong tea' for what seemed like ages, then across to the fire, then along the explosive-blackened walls, before looking into his host's eyes and replying: 'I teach'.

And it was the right answer. The only answer. The one that enabled us make a polite farewell and drive back to Dublin with our kneecaps intact.

And it is true. That is what Bill Richardson loved to do. To teach and write, write and teach, for sixty years of his academic life, mentoring and forming over three generations of students. Many of us are gathered in this chapel today in Campion where Bill passed away three days ago, the new history of St Ignatius and Tom Sheehan's *Making Sense of Heidegger* by his bedside (Tom was his first student and the last to visit before he died). And during all those years of masterful pedagogy, Bill was as challenging and he was inspiring. For every time he commented NG (no good) or MA (what do the Medievals say?) in the margins of an essay, he invariably added: 'You can do it — encore!'

One last memory. When Anne and I visited Bill shortly before he died, we joked about the many times he came to dinner in our house and would feed our dog, Maisie, camembert and crackers under the table. Maisie adored Bill and would wag her entire body in excitement every time he came to the door, knowing what was in store. I used to tease Bill that it was his Superego feeding his Id. And he would laugh. For his 96th birthday in November, I gave him a card of the faithfully departed Maisie with a mouth full of golf balls. When it was time for a last goodbye, Bill lay back in his bed, card in hand, and gave one of his deep silent shuddering chuckles, and whispered 'Bon Appétit'.

I have no doubt that Bill is now enjoying a good meal of camembert and crackers with Maisie, his sister Peg and other departed loved ones.

'Bon appétit Bill!'

As they say in Irish,
> 'His likes will never be seen again'
> *Ní beidh a leithéid ann arís*.

Richard Kearney,
Professor of Philosophy
Boston College

DANIEL DAHLSTROM

I will never forget Bill's kindness towards me, the twinkle in his eyes when he was laughing or making a point (suggesting I take a second look at a text or, better, read what it says!). Like all my colleagues in the Heidegger Circle, I benefited in more ways than can said or imagined from the uncanny sweep and depth of his knowledge of Heidegger's thinking. But we also benefited, even more importantly, from his sheer presence among us, a presence that was serene but hardly laid-back, the presence of a spirit both tough and generous, earthy and worldly. (I have only one criticism of Bill: his driving. There's something called 'a Boston stop,' that can perhaps be explained by the rotaries around Beantown. But then there's the 'Richardson go-and-don't stop,' that means keep moving unless an immovable object or the laws of physics — forget traffic signs — prevent you.)

Bill welcomed me into the Heidegger circle over a quarter of a century ago. I particularly appreciated that support at the time since I did not know many Heidegger scholars, not having the pedigree of someone who studied Heidegger or phenomenology at one of the major schools. But he went out of his way to make it clear to me that this did not matter.

At a SPEP session on a recent work by a prominent and popular Heidegger scholar who was a friend of Bill, I harshly criticized what I took to be unsupportable claims about analytical approaches to ethics and the history of modern ethics made by the scholar. At the break at the end of the talk before the scholar is given the opportunity to respond, there was considerable commotion and head-shaking; the tension in the air was obvious; I remember feeling more than a little isolated at the moment. I was on my way to the restroom during the break when, out of the blue, Bill grabs me and, smiling broadly, says something like "don't take too long; you've got to be here when he tries to answer those blows." Even if we disagreed on this or that point, Bill gave me the sense that he had my back (as well as his friend's) and that the Sache selbst is what mattered. Several years later, he came alone to my presidential address on "Negation and Being" at the Metaphysical Society of America, sitting in the back, his head leaning downward, barely propped up in his hand. Despite its Heideggerian echoes, the talk made no mention of Heidegger. During the talk I glanced occasionally in Bill's direction, worrying that he was either falling asleep or simply aghast that I would give such a paper to metaphysicians! But towards the end of the talk, he lifted up his head, raising his eyebrows, and flashed that broad, knowing smile of his in my direction. He gave me that same smile at Weston in early December, laughing at stories of my misbegotten youth before finally shaking my hand and whispering "thanks for coming," two days before he left us.

Daniel Dahlstrom
Professor of Philosophy
Boston University

PINA MONETA

Dear Bill,[3]

As this life moves towards its twilight, profiles of ruins accompany my steps. Theories have come and gone; open and closed systems have crumbled; dismantling and deconstruction have reduced foundations to dust, and along with it, all possibilities of foundation. The latest wars have swept away the tenuous hope that reason, human reason, may have a chance to govern human affairs. And yet, among ruins large and small, cornerstone fragments are still to be found. To look

---

[3] Giuseppina Moneta, "Profile" in: Babich, ed., *From Phenomenology to Thought, Errancy, and Desire: Essays in Honor of William J. Richardson, S.J.* [Phænomenologica] (Kluwer Academic Publishers. Dordrecht. 1995), pp. 205-207.

for them and hold them in sight for a brief while is not without significance; it may lead to origins of sense and meanings still there however precariously and it may offer an occasion, as it does now, for gratitude. ...

Pina Moneta and Bill Richardson, Six Fours, France, Summer 2009

Fragments I call here dialogues. Our dialogues, Bill, began long ago. I shall try to say here something I have learned from them as an apprentice in the craft of philosophical reflection.

In those talks, I recall, the dialogue, as an experience of the spoken word, began to appear as something other than a meeting or encounter, and even less a sharing of selves, as is usually and meaninglessly said. Rather it was an event having to do with space, or, I better say, with emptiness. The strange relationship between the spoken and the soundless spacing surrounding it was brought into focus by a listening of a new sort, or, I better say, by a learning to listen. ...

But there was still another sort of spacing in those dialogues we had, which led to my listening to another dimension of awareness. No doubt it was a mental game I engaged in at the time, elicited by the vacuum first encountered, as an announced presence demanding further attention. It meant an invitation to attend to other sorts of spacings. These were the soundless distances between words and sentences. The listening shifted to these intervals of muteness.

Contrary to what may have appeared, these spacings were not interruptions, or stretches of silence, or blanks. They were rather perceived on a continuum with the spoken. Disseminated throughout the discourse, these pauses and intervals called for attention, as having an immediate and essential relation to the spoken.

The fact is that the two, the spoken and the emptiness surrounding it, appeared as a homogenous phenomenon. Emptiness was not a blank but a stretching out of the spoken: the range and horizon of its resonance. Emptiness in other words had its own efficacy. It had the active power of making the spoken transparent and pulling it towards wider depths. The spacing before and after the verbal expression began to appear as still hidden, unformulated possibilities of the spoken, as the place of provenance and indefinite, still undecided meanings.

It became clear that my attention to the relationshiop, begun in curiosity, between the spoken and the emptiness surrounding it had revealed the possibility of another listening. I had learned the first step in getting rid of "the habit of always hearing only what we already understand."...

Giuseppina Moneta
Professor *emerita*
of Philosophy
John Cabot University,
Rome, Italy

Bill Richardson, S.J and Patrick Aidan Heelan, S.J.
Six-Fours, France, 2009

ROBERT INNIS

Bill knew how to hold a glass — and ask for a refill. In 1969 on a very hot summer day he came to dinner at our apartment in the Bronx. He arrived a bit later than the others, who were not 'quiet folk' and were making sufficient noise to indicate they were having a good time. My wife, Marianne, asked him what he would like to drink and in the midst of the din heard him mumble something the last word of which was 'water.' So, somewhat perplexed, she gave him a glass of water. Seeing after a while that the glass was practically empty, she asked him if he wanted a refill. He smiled and said, yes he would, but could she go a bit heavier with the scotch this time.

Robert Innis,
Professor *emeritus*
of Philosophy
University of
Massachusetts, Lowell

RICHARD BOOTHBY

"But could she go a bit heavier on the scotch this time." What a quintessential Bill joke.

Surely one of the most fitting and eloquent tributes to Bill is precisely this circle of friends and colleagues, including especially his students, who here celebrate their memories and reflections of him. We will carry forward the fully living Bill Richardson for the rest of our lives, not just in those memories of him that cannot fail to bring a smile, but even more so for the gift he gave as an exemplar of the craft of thinking. I can see and hear now with perfect vividness the thing I most honored in him: the exquisitely sensitive touch with which he would take up an idea, turning it now this way and now that, as if handling a breathlessly fragile piece of antique porcelain. Then, at a certain point, inconceivably, those Irish eyes would increase their sparkle as he would bear down with a quiet ferocity on some point that particularly moved him. That moment of intensity would finally pass like a summer squall and he would pause, as if giving us all a little respite, and punctuate his discourse with a gentle joke, often aimed at himself. It was a lesson not in any particular concept but in the manner in which a genuine thinker lives his vocation. I will remain forever grateful to have been witness to it.

Richard Boothby
Professor of Philosophy
Loyola University,
Maryland

JEFFREY BLOECHL

Last summer I went to see Bill in Campion late one morning. He was, as you all know, an eager host: "Can I offer you something to drink?" I looked at my watch, but he beat me to it: "If I take my time getting things in order, it will be 12 by the time I pour you a good glass." He was not to have any, on doctor's orders, and that pained him. After handing me my glass, he said, "I think if I were to put a good amount of water in my glass, and just a few drops of scotch, that can't do any harm." We settled in with our glasses. Some minutes later, a nurse came in: "What is that in your glass, Father?" Bill slid the glass down out of sight, between his chair and the wall. "There is water in my glass." You can guess what came next, as she left the room: "Strictly speaking, what I said was true."

….

Ok, I can't resist adding a funny one, too. Bill and I co-taught Lacan's sixth seminar some years ago. It contains a lengthy and difficult interpretation of Hamlet, which led us into efforts to get at the play in our own terms. I figured I had it sorted out for myself one day, and at some point during our next seminar meeting elaborated at some length while Bill listened, chin on chest, to my immediate left. "That's all and good, except for the fact that that's not exactly how Shakespeare wrote it." And there followed, as if from up his sleeve, a series of minor discrepancies that together destroyed my reading of the play. Rigor and fidelity to the details mattered a great deal when Bill was about serious matters.

Jeffrey Bloechl
Associate Professor
of Philosophy
Boston College

SCOTT M. CAMPBELL

Fr. Richardson was always "Fr. Richardson" to me. I never called him "Bill," even though I knew him for over twenty years. In graduate school at Boston College, a friend told me that I had to take Richardson's class, "The Later Heidegger." Until that time, my only exposure to Heidegger was through a course on "Hegel to Derrida" taught by Richard Rorty at the University of Virginia. When Fr. Richardson found this out, he asked me to give a presentation to the class on Rorty's reading of Heidegger. After I was finished, Fr. Richardson said, "But that's not philosophy. Rorty is not doing philosophy."

Was he angry? He sounded so to my twenty-one year old ears, but what I came to realize was that to him, it mattered. Philosophy mattered, and Heidegger mattered. Being mattered.

He did not immediately agree to work with me on my dissertation. I approached him tentatively with a topic on Heidegger's use of metaphor in the *Beiträge* and asked him to direct it. He responded, "In principle, yes." Was that actually a yes? Was it a qualified yes? What did it mean? Later that semester, another graduate student defended a dissertation on Husserl and Heidegger, and Fr. Richardson was at the defense. He said, "But what about Heidegger's notion of facticity — as we see it in his lectures on the early Christians — where life and death are right on your doorstep." While speaking, he waved his arms and moved his hands here and there, while modulating his voice for emphasis.

The intensity of this performance made me want to write on facticity, and when I approached him again with that topic, this time with conviction, he agreed. He did not want to read chapters as I wrote them. He told me to work independently, as he had done himself, writing his book on Heidegger at a monastery in the Black Forest. So, two years later, I brought him 300 pages. He served me dinner, and we walked through my rough draft page by page for over seven hours. His advice improved the work significantly, and I defended in 1999. I was the last student to write a dissertation with him.

He once celebrated a mass with Paul Bruno and me. Instead of delivering a homily, he suggested that the three of us talk about the nature of truth for a while. Our discussion meandered from truth to religion to family to God. After the mass, he offered us coffee and cake, and we discussed his work on Lacan. He shared with us a dream that he had had while completing his own psychoanalysis in Paris: He was driving through Brooklyn when his car broke down, on Church Street. [He noted the irony.] In the dream, he said, in French, *"J'ai besoin d'essence*" ("I need gas") but in the context of analysis, this also meant "*J'ai besoin de sens*" ("I need meaning").

Fr. Richardson presided at my wedding in 2010. My wife and I had an abbreviated Pre-Cana meeting with him, where we also discussed the wedding service itself. He insisted that we try to be brief and not go longer than an hour. We told everyone involved to stick to the schedule. Then, Fr. Richardson delivered a 45-minute homily. 45 minutes! But time is a vulgar concept. I loved every second of that homily. It was personal; it was philosophical; it was Heideggerian. He did not stick to the schedule, but he gave a performance that meant something. The last time I saw Fr. Richardson, we had dinner together with Paul Bruno and Ed McGushin at an Italian family-style restaurant in Waltham, MA. He was frail, and after dinner, Paul and I instinctively tried to help him up the stairs at the Campion Center where he was living. He shrugged off our help, and with one hand gingerly holding the handrail, he glided up the stairs by himself.

Scott M. Campbell
Professor and Chair of Philosophy
Nazareth College

DIETER BRUMM

Bill Richardson's friend from his student days in Freiburg, the journalist, philosopher, and poet, Dieter Brumm, pictured here in Tübingen, Spring, 1997.

Dieter sent me a memorial reflection after a friendship that lasted more than 60 years.

Die Freundschaft mit WILLIAM J. RICHARDSON, SJ hat mein Leben über sechzig Jahre lang mitbestimmt und mitgestaltet. Wie kein anderer Philosoph hat er durch seine tiefe Menschlichkeit, seine Selbstlosigkeit und die Offenheit seines Denkens meinen eigenen Weg begleitet und vertieft.

Er war — wie auch ich — in den 50er Jahren nach Freiburg gekommen, um die Philosophie Martin Heideggers zu studieren, dessen Werk *Sein und Zeit* schon 1926 erschienen, aber erst nach dem Krieg intensiver diskutiert worden war; er lehrte noch in Freiburg. RICHARDSONS Auseinandersetzung mit dessen Denken erschien 1963 unter dem Titel *Through Phenomenology to Thought*. Wie sehr Heidegger selbst die eigenständige und keineswegs unkritische Interpretation seines Werkes schätzte, machte er mit seinem Vorwort zu diesem Buch deutlich: „Mein Wunsch ist es, Ihr Werk...möge helfen, das mehrfältige Denken der einfachen und deshalb die Fülle bergenden Sache des Denkens in Gang zu bringen".Das bestätigt auch eine Anekdote, die RICHARDSON der vierten Auflage seines Buches 2003 voranstellte. Nach einem intensiv vorbereiteten Gespräch mit Heidegger habe dieser seinen Kollegen, den Philosophieprofessor Max Müller, gefragt : „Wer ist denn dieser Kerl? Soviele haben mich mißverstanden, aber hier ist einer, der mein Denken begriffen hat — und das ist ausgerechnet ein Amerikaner!"

Mit BILL RICHARDSON S.J., dem Philosophen und wohl besten Interpreten des Denkers Martin Heidegger, habe ich meinen ältesten Freund verloren, dessen bescheidene Uneigennützigkeit ein Fanal gegen allen Größenwahn und schrankenlosen Egoismus der Epoche gesetzt hat. *Requiescat in pace*!

Dieter Brumm
Hamburg

Bill Richardson, Messkirch, May 2015

BABETTE BABICH

It occurred to me to edit a Festschrift collection for Bill Richardson — which I assembled quite against his wishes, as Bill took some care to have me understand.

The effort cost me time *and* a job opportunity *and* a fellowship, all that ontic stuff. But Bill was a scholar who should have, if anyone should have (and many have these with lesser reason), a Festschrift.

My introduction was added at the last moment (I just listed all the things going on by way of noting the deficits), and began with the words from Hölderlin, *Wie du anfiengst, wirst du bleiben.*

The Festschrift itself would move him considerably, he glowed with joy at the gloriously festive dinner organized by his fellow New Yorker and friend, Father Leo O'Donovan, S.J., in his honor at Georgetown University's Riggs Library and he treasured the special volume Kluwer prepared for him, having it bound in red leather.

Bill Richardson, with the author and Bill's sister, Peg Powers, 1995. Festive Dinner for a Fedstschrift, Riggs Library, Georgetown

WILLIAM J. RICHARDSON, S.J., REFLECTIONS 31

Bill Richardson. S.J. and Leo O'Donovan, S.J.
Festive Dinner for a Festschrift, Georgetown, 1995

A lot of people contributed to that *Festschrift*, literally from A to Z — John Anderson on Mark Twain and Plato's Laws to Slavoj Žižek on Lacan. In addition to Tom Sheehan and Richard Capobianco, it was a Heideggerian who's who: Joan Stambaugh and Friedrich von Hermann, Michael Theunissen, Max Müller, Pina Moneta, Karsten Harries, Fred Dallmayr, Ted Kisiel, Graeme Nicholson, Joseph Kockelmans, Patrick Heelan, Adriaan Peperzak, Sam IJsseling, Al Lingis, Debra Bergoffen, Jack Caputo, Robert Bernasconi, and Richard Kearney and the late David Allison. I invited Žižek to be sure we had a good cadre of Lacanians, like Rick Boothby, to match the

Heideggerians. It was an overlong book, including an essay I found questionable but because Bill favored its author, I left in all its uncut glory.

I published two of Bill's own essays in his Festschrift and Bill went on to write a quasi-review of it, himself: "From Phenomenology through Thought to a Festschrift" for the 1997 issue of *Heidegger Studies*.

Holderlin's rhythmic line, *as you began, you will stay*, includes the gyre of becoming. I say 'gyre' because when I caught a ride from Boston to New York Bill would play *Books on Tape*. I brought Sophocles but Bill preferred Yeats. And the gyre we know because all of us are caught in it.

Bill liked those cassettes because he loved the spken word but also, perhaps mostly, to keep from falling asleep, which to my alarm, Bill would do frequently while driving. He never had an accident (not that I knew of) yet in later years he drove in sinewaves, schussing across *both* directions of traffic in the streets of Newton and Brookline: it was clear to everyone (but not to Bill) that he should not drive.

Unlike most grad students at Boston College, I never took Tom Owens' two semester course on *Being and Time*. I had read Bill's book at Stony Brook, immediately upon finishing *Being and Time* — wanting more Heidegger and that 'more' was

Bill's book. I took all the courses Gadamer offered, so too Taminiaux and Lonergan. In the same way, I took all the courses Bill offered, whether I was interested in the theme or not, whether useful for my research or not.

Bill's tastes in philosophy (with the patent exception of Heidegger) differed radically from my own which meant I couldn't ask Bill to direct my dissertation. So I asked Jacques Taminiaux and Bill took that as an insult. Because Taminiaux was famously forgiving, I thought Bill would give me a hard time with my text (I was right about this and he did this with dedication for the rest of his life), I asked him to be a reader. Bill took that as a second insult. He paid me back during my defense, why was it that, given that I took care to quote Pindar in the original Greek and Nietzsche in the original German and Jean Granier in the original French, I had not arranged to quote the original Aramaic? The question baffles me to this day. But Bill was not joking.

When SPEP asked him to comment on my book, *Words in Blood, Like Flowers* his words were so savage (the book is about Heidegger, Hölderlin, and, alas, for me: Nietzsche) that a friend who knew us both, shook her head, saying Bill had gone too far, and suggesting that I would be at fault if I continued to have anything to do with him thereafter. It is not that I was not hurt still I understood that Bill's criticisms were based on a failure to understand my work and, to my mind, part of the responsibility for understanding an author lies with the reader who is sovereign in this respect. It is not as if I supposed there was nothing wrong with anything I wrote but Bill never got that far: he worried the first point he found: "*Nietzsche hat mich kaput gemacht*" and criticized my translation for the better part of an hour, which translation happened *not* to be wrong. Only at the end of his life did Bill begin to concede that Nietzsche was significant for Heidegger's thought.

Despite Nietzsche, despite our different takes on doing philosophy, we were extremely close friends. Bill met my family and always asked about them, especially my youngest brother Tihomil, I helped him (he required constant advice literally from the moment I met him which, as a second year graduate student, I found perplexing), I built things for him, set up computers for him, helped him organize projects, discussed his papers, helped organize and shop and arrange dinner parties for friends, including an obsession with crème brûlée, complete with tiny flame throwers and other plans for a respectable crust and there was one glorious tarte tatin cooked over the length of an afternoon in Carlisle. I drank sherry (I hate sherry) and talked long hours on the phone with him — *where are you,* he would invariably ask, taking care to enunciate the words. His meaning was clear but, especially in later years, my answer nearly always meant I was not close at hand. I visited with him in New York, or better said: he visited me. I traveled with him in Europe, meeting him in Paris, Germany, including several visits to Messkirch, Todtnauberg, and a pilgrimage, despite everything, to Nietzsche's Sils Maria, as well as Italy, summer weeks in the South of France, and again, for one last time, two years ago, to Messkirch: collecting Bill from the Zurich airport to drive him to the Black Forest and back again to Zurich. And yet it should be said, I was not part of Bill's inner circle, decided as these things are by others. And these inner circles were many and various: Bill was an astonishing number of things to a lot of people.

The last time I spoke in any extended way with Bill, a good two weeks before he died, was the day before I flew to Italy for a conference in Cassino, very fittingly, on the theme of "Violence." I recall standing outside in late November on the Fordham campus at Rose Hill where Bill had taught, and told him when he asked that I was calling from the lawn just in sight of Collins Hall,

We spoke of the campus, of the sky, the Fordham students, we spoke of Italy, he remembered Cassino, and that reminded him of Rome and of

Pina Moneta and I murmured her frustration in trying to call him, and, again, I said, his friend, Dieter Brumm had written just a few days before to ask again for his email for the second time that month in those days of difficult contact. I had already told him all this. Bill was delighted to hear it: again: did Dieter write? Oh, yes. And he laughed and I laughed.

Bill found my style of writing too hard to read: back in the eighties he explained that he did not think he should have to 'work' to read someone other than Heidegger (hard to argue with that). Yet if his objections never induced me to write in the simple fashion Bill thought philosophy should approximate, our friendship was nothing like Bill's ideal for writing but closer to mine: complicatedly wrought with deep undercurrents and abiding admiration.

Babette Babich
Professor of Philosophy
Fordham University

GRAEME NICHOLSON

Bill Richardson was, to me, not only the author of the great book on Heidegger and numerous eloquent articles, but the most effective speaker I know among modern academics — which this anecdote may illustrate.

At a meeting of SPEP sometime in the '80's, Bill gave a talk on Jacques Lacan (whom I had never read), that completely swept me away. « And the mother says, 'oohh, ton père!!' Le NOM du père est LE NON du père. » Inspired, I immediately ordered a book by Lacan for my coming Philosophy class. I had no time to study it until a week before class. I was puzzled that a book in English would have the title *ECRITS*, but then I began to read it, and found each article utterly incomprehensible, and despaired over the course meetings that were looming up. But it turned out that the students were thrilled that an instructor had assigned their favorite author, and competed with each other for the opportunity to make class presentations on Lacan. Thus I sat back and listened to their presentations, and by the end of the semester I too had become something of a Lacanian.

Graeme Nicholson
Professor *emeritus*
of Philosophy
University of Toronto

RICHARD CAPOBIANCO

In conversations to the very end, Bill gratefully recalled Heidegger's generosity and graciousness, and he ever remained struck by how profoundly calm and meditative Heidegger became in peering out into the wooded landscape — it was the countenance of a "nature mystic" in Bill's words.

There is really so much to say about the achievement that is Bill's book, yet simply consider just this: When he was finally finished with his painstaking research, his initial manuscript was more than 1,100 typewritten pages in length. Every page a model of philosophical rigor and clarity.

His opening words to the main part of his great book continue to tell us as much about Bill's way over the course of his lifetime as about Heidegger's way. Here's what he wrote:

> *There is a long and winding way that leads from Reichenau to Todtnauberg. It is Martin Heidegger's way. Past the moor and through the fields, it wends its way over the hills, only to wander now this way, now that, along uncharted forest trails. Yet for all its meandering, it moves in a single direction; it is but a single way. The purpose of these pages is*

to trace in some measure that way in order to raise the question whether others may walk it too.[4]

Richard Capobianco
Professor of Philosophy
Stonehill College

JEAN GRONDIN

Father Richardson was a towering, even mythical figure for Heidegger readers. His truly seminal book, *Through Phenomenology to Thought*, as well as Heidegger's own letter-preface to this book, known throughout the world as the « Letter to Richardson », were primary sources for all. This letter, which was a second « Letter on Humanism » with its clarifications about the *Kehre*, showed Heidegger at his didactic best, thoughtfully answering questions from an insightful young student. Heidegger himself viewed this Letter as an essential document since he read it in a seminar with his students.

---

[4] From remarks offered at the Heidegger Circle, 2016.

It is remarkable that Heidegger took a liking to an American commentator of his work, especially in light of what he says about America in his Black Notebooks and elsewhere. Father Richardson's book had demonstrated to the world, and I am sure to Heidegger himself, that American philosophers were not a bunch of hopeless logical positivists, but could be very careful readers and first-rate thinkers.

To my knowledge, this preface is the only one Heidegger ever wrote for a book published in English. Besides the obvious merits of the study, in which Heidegger probably heralded a minute reading of his work that he could not find in Germany, it probably helped that Father Richardson was a priest and a Jesuit. In spite of his rantings about Catholics, in his Notebooks for instance, Heidegger had a genuine sympathy for many Catholic priests and philosophers such as Karl Rahner, Max Müller, Bernhard Welte, Karl Lehmann or Father Richardson. Perhaps he saw in them an image of what he could have become had he not « strayed » on his own path through phenomenology to thought.

I fondly recall my first meeting with Father Richardson. It was in the fall of 1992 when John Cleary kindly invited me to give two talks on Gadamer at Boston College. Given Gadamer's long presence as a guest lecturer at Boston College, I had expected to meet some Gadamer pupils, but to my surprise there were not many there besides John Cleary.

I was introduced however to an older, elegant, delicate and well-mannered gentleman called Bill Richardson. Bill who? I had to brush my eyes, realizing after a moment of stupor that it was *the* William Richardson I had been reading for so many years, the author of an indispensable summa of Heidegger's main works (i.e., those he published himself and which are philosophically far superior to the many manuscripts he chose not to publish) and the recipient of Heidegger's letter, the American Beaufret, as it were.

I hadn't expected that he was still teaching or that, if he happened to be in Boston, he would bother to attend my talks. He patiently did and asked pointed, benevolent and simple questions that always went to the heart of the matter.

During my visit, he also had the generosity to invite me to a restaurant on Boston Harbour. Late into the night, we spoke of the charms of Boston, the difference between Bostoners and New Yorkers, and of course about Gadamer, Heidegger, his encounter with him, the turn and the new Heidegger affair that had arose after the publication of Farias' book and on which Father

Richardson had just written a thoughtful piece, but about which he was unsure.

He had a very open mind on all matters and was very affable. I immediately understood why Gadamer, with whom he had shared so many discussions, spoke of him with such praise. It was also obvious why Heidegger took a liking to him, writing a generous letter on the core issues of his thinking to such an exceptional hermeneutic. Philosophy was very lucky to have him and I am sure this is especially true of his students.

Jean Grondin
Professor of Philosophy
Université de Montréal, Canada

PAUL BRUNO, ED McGUSHIN, AND SCOTT CAMPBELL

It took a while for Bill to commit to cooperating in the making of a documentary film about his intellectual life.[5] When the filming finally ended, we thanked him for his patience, honesty, and commitment. His reply was a wave and an off-

---

[5] See bibliography below, for further detail: pp. 110-111.

handed remark: "Well, in for a penny, in for a pound."

When we were discussing making a documentary film about Bill, we knew that our most difficult task was going to be getting Bill to allow us to do it. We all agreed that we would not pursue the project without Bill's permission. To say that Bill was reluctant when we first broached the subject with him would be an understatement. He was vaguely dismissive at first, making it clear that this kind of project was something young people — people of "your generation"— spend time doing. He suggested that no one would be particularly interested in watching such a film. What for?

It was during a follow-up telephone conversation with Ed that Bill reluctantly agreed to do a first interview on camera. Shortly after that interview, we told Bill that we planned on going to SPEP in Memphis in order to interview a number of his former students. The thought of his former students talking about him seemed to raise his level of distress a bit, but again, he went along with it. When we saw him in the lobby at the hotel in Memphis, we briefly told him the names of those we scheduled for interviews. At best, he grunted.

A couple of hours later, Scott answered the phone in our hotel room, and after his initial "Hello," Scott said aloud, "Hi, Father." Would this be the call that pulled the plug on the entire project? Instead, Scott hung up the phone, turned toward us, and in an imitation of Bill's hushed vocal tone, said, "Scott, you know I find all this business personally distasteful, but I thought you would want to know that Vincent McCarthy is at the conference, and he would be a good person to interview."

Paul Bruno
Associate Professor of Philosophy
Framingham State College

Scott M. Campbell
Professor of Philosophy
Nazareth College, Rochester

Edward F. McGushin
Associate Professor of Philosophy
Stonehill College

THOMAS SHEEHAN

In memoriam William J. Richardson, S.J. (1920-2016)[6]

ἀνδρός, ὡς ἡμεῖς φαῖμεν ἄν,
τῶν τότε ὧν ἐπειράθημεν
ἀρίστου καὶ ἄλλως φρονιμωτάτου καὶ δικαιοτάτου.

---

[6] These paragraphs are taken from a longer piece that will be published in French next month.

Professor William J. Richardson, S.J. — the brilliant philosopher and writer, psychoanalyst and teacher, mentor and friend to two generations of students and colleagues — died on 10 December 2016, at the beginning of his 97th year, in Weston, Massachusetts.

Richardson's masterwork, *Heidegger: Through Phenomenology to Thought* (1963), was the first treatise in any language to present a comprehensive interpretation of the *whole* of Heidegger's work as it was known up through the late 1950s. Written with a clarity and precision that few have managed to imitate, that 800-page tome radically shifted how scholars came to view Heidegger: no longer as an existentialist in the mold of Jean-Paul Sartre but rather as a philosopher in pursuit of the elusive "X," *die Sache selbst*, that enables and requires us to understand the so-called "being" of things, that is, their current significance in the worlds of our lived concerns.

Born in Brooklyn in 1920, William J. Richardson attended Holy Cross College, Worchester, Massachusetts from 1937 to 1941, where, along with a brilliant curriculum, he was noted for his consummate theatrical skills, both as Shakespeare's Richard II and as Sophocles' Antigone in a performance of the tragedy entirely in Greek.

Upon graduation, he entered the Society of Jesus at the seminary in Poughkeepsie, New York, and thereafter followed the typical process of Jesuit formation:

> 1941-43, novitiate
> 1943-44, juniorate
> 1944-47, licentiate in philosophy: Woodstock College, Maryland
> 1947-50, regency: teaching English and philosophy at Le Moyne College, Syracuse
> 1950-54, licentiate in theology: Collège Saint-Albert, Eegenhoven-Louvain
> 1953, ordination to the priesthood
> 1954-55, tertianship, in Austria.

Richardson's desire was to go on to take a doctorate in theology under Karl Rahner, S.J. (1904-1984), who was teaching in Innsbruck and had just begun publishing his multi-volume *Schriften zur Theologie.* In a personal meeting with Rahner during his year of tertianship, However, Richardson's superiors decided against that path and insisted that instead he take the Ph.D. in philosophy so as to eventually teach metaphysics in the United States. Having matriculated (none too happily) at Louvain's Institut Supérieur de Philosophie and chosen (quite happily) Alphonse de Waelhens as his supervisor, Richardson obtained permission to spend the first semester of his graduate studies — autumn of 1955 — at Freiburg

University, where Heidegger would be lecturing on *Der Satz vom Grund* (now GA 10).

Richardson had little familiarity with Heidegger's work at the time, but he was searching for a dissertation topic in metaphysics and knew that Heidegger was interested in that issue.

While attending Heidegger's lecture course that fall, Richardson met a young Jesuit from Rome, Father Virgilio Fagone, who was among a dozen or so select participants in Heidegger's seminar on Hegel, which was meeting that semester at Heidegger's home. It was from the ever enthusiastic Fagone that Richardson first heard of *die Kehre*, the alleged "reversal" in Heidegger's thought in the 1930s. This was issue that became central to Richardson's own interpretation of Heidegger.

One Friday afternoon in the late fall of 1955, Richardson summoned up the courage to approach Heidegger during his office hours and, in halting German, to ask his opinion on three possible dissertation topics. Would a comparison of Husserl's and Heidegger's phenomenology be advisable? No, said Heidegger, that's far too large a topic. How about the ontological difference? Another "no," because Heidegger had much more yet to publish on that. Then what about *Seinsdenken*, understood as "foundational thought" [*das wesentliche Denken*] in the later work — would that be a suitable dissertation topic? As Richardson later wrote, Heidegger responded with "a firm *Ja*."

But when he returned to Louvain in early 1956, Richardson ran into opposition in the person of his dissertation director. "Are you *serious*?" asked de Waelhens. "Do you really want to work on *that*?" De Waelhens' own book, *La philosophie de Martin Heidegger* (1942), had focused only on Heidegger's early work, and he was convinced that the later Heidegger had abandoned philosophy for something verging on poetry. But with Heidegger's firm "Yes" backing him up, Richardson persisted, and de Waelhens finally agreed to supervise the dissertation. Working steadily for the next three years, partly in Louvain but mostly at a Benedictine convent in the Black Forest, Richardson produced a manuscript of no less than 1,100 typed pages and some 5,000 footnotes, all of which, as he came to see by 1959 and in his own words, "sabotaged" de Waelhens' interpretation of Heidegger. And yet, in full awareness that such was the case, de Waelhens generously encouraged his student throughout, even if he occasionally suggested *"un peu de distance, quand même."*

The dissertation completed, Richardson sent Heidegger a 25-page summary of the manuscript, which the philosopher read closely and marked up extensively. In February of 1959, in a four-hour meeting at Heidegger's home in Freiburg — the only extended encounter between the two — the Master approved the text with only two minor corrections.[7] As Richardson found out the next day, Heidegger telephoned their mutual friend Max Müller to marvel that someone *finally* understood him — and it was an *American*! Richardson returned to Louvain, presented the first half of the manuscript to the faculty, and successfully defended it in the spring of 1960.

Invited to apply for the maître agrégé at Louvain, Richardson spent the next two years preparing the final version of his master work, which in 1962 he successfully defended (in three languages) before a panel that included Emmanuel Levinas, Paul Ricoeur, and Alphonse de Waehlens. Following their meeting in 1959 Heidegger had agreed in principle to write a preface to the eventual book, and in April of 1962, when the manuscript was already in press, Heidegger penned his now famous response to two questions from Richardson — about the origins of his *Seinsfrage* and about *die Kehre* — while carefully noting at the end of his text that

---

[7] Heidegger suggested that in the subtitle Richardson substitute "*Through* Phenomenology to Thought" for the original subtitle "*From* Phenomenology to Thought" and that he use *Subjektität* rather than *Subjectivität* when discussing Leibniz.

"you alone bear the responsibility" for the work. That letter became the Preface to *Heidegger: Through Phenomenology to Thought*, which appeared (but only after some difficulties stirred up by Hermann Van Breda had been settled) in early 1963.

In his later years, over a glass or two of Scotch, Richardson would recount how, when he returned to the States still smarting from the decision that had denied him a Ph.D. in theology, he visited the Jesuit superior who had made that decision. Without further ado, Richardson dropped the 764-page book on the superior's desk and said, "You wanted a philosophy book? Here's your philosophy book."

In 1963 Richardson was assigned to teach philosophy to Jesuit seminarians at Shrub Oak, New York, but after a single, not uncontroversial year (those were the days of the Second Vatican Council, not to mention the Sixties), he was somewhat brusquely transferred out.

In 1965, following a year's sabbatical, he was appointed to the philosophy department of Fordham University in the Bronx. His seminars on Heidegger, which I was privileged to attend for three years, were extraordinary exercises in close reading and rigorously honed questions posed by a master teacher who often exhausted himself preparing for the weekly meetings. He was always harder on himself than he ever was on any student, but his criticisms, often understated, could be devastating. (His laconic response to my first term paper was a single sentence as he handed the essay back: "Well, if that's the best you can do, I guess that's the best you can do.")

It was during the Fordham years (1965-80) that Richardson deepened his interest in what he termed the "philosophical foundations of psychoanalysis," especially with regard to the human subject, desire, and ethics. From 1969 through 1974 he reduced his philosophy teaching at Fordham in order to take the Certificate in Psychoanalysis from the William Alanson White Institute in New York City, while also conducting research at the Austen Riggs Center in Stockbridge, Massachusetts. Both institutions were founded by Erich Fromm, Clara Thompson, and Harry Stack Sullivan, with strong influence from Sándor Ferenczi's "active" therapeutics and Erik Erikson's ego psychology.

Early in his term as Director of Research at Austen Riggs (1974-1979), and while still teaching at Fordham, Richardson discovered the work of Jacques Lacan. He attended Lacan's lectures at Yale and Columbia in November and December of 1975 and decided that in order to understand what he was saying, he would have to undergo Lacanian psychoanalysis. In 1978 Richardson met with Lacan in Paris and during the next year-and-a-half underwent analysis with one of Lacan's associates. Two books emerged from these experiences and research, both written with his colleague John P. Muller: *Lacan and Language: A Reader's Guide to the Ecrits* (1982; French translation, *Ouvrir les Ecrits de Jacques Lacan,* 1987) and the co-edited *The Purloined Poe: Lacan, Derrida, and Psychoanalytic Reading* (1988).

In 1980, Richardson unhappily terminated his connection with Fordham University. He was then invited to take a position as professor of philosophy at Boston College, Newton, Massachusetts, where his colleagues included Hans Georg Gadamer, Jacques Taminiaux, and [later] Richard Kearney. He taught courses in Heidegger, Lacan, and ethics and continued his psychoanalytic practice until he retired in 2007.

But what to say not about Bill Richardson the scholar but about the man I knew and loved?

At the request of Bill's colleague, Jeff Bloechl, I wrote a few words to be read at his wake and funeral, which I was unable to attend:

FOR BILL RICHARDSON

Of Socrates' death Plato writes, "We wept not for him but for ourselves, for being deprived of such a friend."

Like Socrates, Bill was both a teacher and a gadfly. He did his teaching not by words so much as by modeling to us how to live authentically and ethically. Yet more than once he cited Heidegger to the effect that teaching does not happen until the student learns.

And as a teacher he was also a gadfly, a provocateur who never wanted to hear his words echoed back to him but always encouraged us to think for ourselves. Once at the end of a seminar at Fordham he cited Nietzsche: "One repays a teacher poorly if one remains only a disciple."

Thus as both teacher and gadfly, his gift to his students was ultimately a task, his *Gabe* an *Aufgabe*.

And as of Plato's Socrates, so too of our own Bill Richardson:

"Of all whom we have known,

he was the best, the wisest, and the most just."

GENE PALUMBO

I first heard of Bill in 1964 from a fellow lay missionary in Baghdad who was teaching at the Jesuit university (Al Hikma) there; I was teaching and coaching at the Jesuit high school (Baghdad College). My friend had graduated from Georgetown, and Bill had given (I think it was) the commencement address to his class. He raved about what a great talk it was. So when I returned to the U.S. to do graduate work in philosophy at Fordham, I looked Bill up. That year he was teaching a two-semester ethics course for seniors at the college. I asked if I could audit it, and he said yes. Can you imagine what it was like to be in his classroom three times a week for two semesters?

A few books were very popular then: Harvey Cox's *Secular City*, Joseph Fletcher's *Situation Ethics*, and John A.T. Robinson's *Honest to God*. Bill devoted a week to each of them at the beginning of the first semester, but then it was, in effect, "Okay, gentlemen, now let's roll up our sleeves," and back we went to the pre-Socratics, working our way from there toward the present.

I could be mistaken, but my impression was that, with the many required courses back then in philosophy and theology, the students felt they'd had more than enough, so anyone who hoped to hold their attention for two more semesters of philosophy had their work cut out for them. But Bill won them over. Near the end of the second semester, during the unit on Heidegger, Bill spoke about Dylan, and one night that semester he gave a lecture on campus on "Heidegger and Dylan." It was extraordinary.

At the end of the semester, the students gave him a lovely beer mug; I think it was made of silver. A while back I reminded Bill of it; into his bedroom he went, and out he came with the mug. The students had engraved, on one side, "To William Richardson: a truly honest man," and on the other, a line from *Hey, Mr. Tambourine Man*: "To dance beneath the diamond sky, with one hand waving free."

...

Something that might be worth mentioning: I remember hearing that one night, not all that long ago, the staff at Campion was very worried because Bill was nowhere to be found. Later that night, he finally showed up. Where had he been? At a Dylan concert. Check it out, just in case it's embellished or apocryphal.[8]

---

[8] The concert evening was 14 November 2015. Richard Kearney confirms: "Thanks for beautiful reflection,

...

I remember a Saturday night in the Bronx when we were somewhere near Fordham, and passed by a television. A boxing match was on the screen. Bill said, "That's my idea of nothing.

PETER LUPARIO

I first met Bill during the 1970–71 academic year when we were both members of the philosophy faculty at Fordham, but did not get to know him at the time. Unable to meet the rapidly growing needs of a young family, I walked out of the academic grove and into the then fledgling thicket of Information Technology.

Having now retired, Ed Reno, a friend and colleague from that year at Fordham, and I jointly decided to return to our roots and renew our

---

Gene, and yes it is true that Bill went AWOL and stole off to Dylan's last big Boston concert with three BC doctoral students, Murray Littlejohn, Marina Denishik and Stephanie Rumpza — and wined and dined them into the wee hours of the mourning. I managed to get a copy of Bill's article on Heidegger and Dylan (which was published in *Philosophy and Social Criticism* two years ago) to Dylan via a friend. Bill was delighted. He had some 'strong tea' in his Dylan Mug to celebrate!"

relationship with Lady Philosophy. We plunged into a close reading of Wilfrid Sellars. And it was in working through his essay on "The Role of Imagination in Kant's Theory of Experience" that bells began to ring. We turned to Heidegger's text on that topic and, of course, to Bill's.

That led us to seek a reconnection with Bill, and under the gracious auspices of Father Madigan and of Jeff Bloechl, we were able to arrange a luncheon meeting with Bill for the end of this past August. When Ed and I arrived, we were informed that Bill had been hospitalized and was unable to have visitors. We remained in touch with Jeff, and when he informed us that Bill was once again strong enough we arranged for another meeting shortly before Bill's birthday. Ed was in Berlin at the time and could not attend, but I was fortunate (blessed?) enough to break bread and to share a few hours of dialogue with Bill. We reminisced a bit (Fordham, Holy Cross, the indelible marks upon the soul thereof ...) before getting into a discussion focused on imagination. While he was certainly frail of body, there was no doubt about his mental acuity. Bill explained that *Kant and the Problem of Metaphysics* provided him with the key to understanding Heidegger.

Our conversation ranged over space/time/imagination, embodiment, pre-linguistic recognition of alterity (twins in the womb!), agency and areas for dialogue with existential Thomism.

Speaking with Bill was as comfortable and pleasant as picking up the conversation where we left off yesterday — even though "yesterday" was more than a few decades ago. I left Bill's room at Campion with the understanding that we would continue the conversation (with Ed, should he be in the US for the holidays) sometime before the New England weather made for treacherous driving. Unfortunately for us, that conversation, if it is to take place at all, will depend upon Ed and I being granted access to the gated community where Bill now resides.

Bill Richardson, at Georgetown University, 1996.

Dieter Jähnig†, Holger Schmid, Babette Babich, Bill Richardson, S.J.†, Überlingen, Lake Constance, 1997.

Photograph by Frau Jähnig.

WILLIAM J. RICHARDSON, S.J., REFLECTIONS

Patrick Aidan Heelan, S.J.†, and Bill Richardson, S.J.†

Patrick Aidan Heelan, S.J.†, Babette Babich,
Bill Richardson. S.J.†, and Leo O'Donovan, S.J.
Riggs Library, Georgetown University, 1996.

St. Martin's Church, Meßkirch, 2015

Breakfast in Meßkirch, 1997

Babette Babich and Bill Richardson, Feldweg, Meßkirch, 1997
Photograph by Holger Schmid, Philosophy, Lille.

ON HEIDEGGER TO LACAN[9]

SH: Mario, would you like to introduce Dr. Richardson?
MB: It's my pleasure to do so. William Richardson was born and raised in the United States and went to Europe, to Belgium, for his doctoral training in philosophy at the Catholic University of Louvain. He was already an internationally known Heidegger scholar in the decade of the 70's when, after training as a psychoanalyst in New York City, he began to interest himself with Jacques Lacan and his return to Freud. Dr Richardson is today a Professor of Philosophy at Boston College as well as a practicing psychoanalyst in Boston where he lives. I will also add that Professor Richardson is a Catholic priest and a member of the Society of Jesus for many years.
My first question concerns his philosophical formation. I've always been curious on why he decided to travel to Europe, and to Louvain in

---

[9] An Interview with William J. Richardson, S. J., Ph.D., with Mario L. Beira Ph.D. & Sara Elena Hassan M.D., psychoanalyst. The interview, an initiative of Dr. Sara Elena Hassan, was conducted on June 21st 2005 in Dublin (Ireland) following an international psychoanalytic conference on Joyce and Lacan. All notes that follow are by Dr Beira.

particular, for his training in philosophy. Secondly, I am wondering if he would be willing to share with us how it was that he decided to do his doctoral dissertation on Heidegger and under the guidance and supervision of Alphonse De Waelhens in particular.

WJR: I originally had hoped to study theology in order to teach theology at an American university. I was then told by my superiors that they needed someone to teach philosophy. So when I went to graduate studies it was with the intention of studying theology. I had done four years of theology at Louvain, at the Faculty of Theology at the Jesuit Seminary, and was told that it would be a good idea to study philosophy in Rome. The Jesuit faculty of theology there had no connection with the university as such so that the university vouched for me in unknown quantity.

I was told by my superiors that I had to be prepared to teach metaphysics in a new seminary being built at that time in the United States. They needed fresh faculty to teach there and I had to be prepared to teach metaphysics. It seemed to me that I could therefore not study theology and that philosophy had then to be studied in a contemporary setting. I learned, almost by accident, that the leading figure and thinker in the area of metaphysics, in whatever sense one may take that, was Martin Heidegger. So I developed at first a casual and indirect interest in Heidegger as a possible subject for research.

At that time the leading specialist in Heidegger studies, in the French language at least, was Alphonse De Waelhens. Professor De Waelhens had published his doctoral dissertation by then. It was an interpretation of *Being and Time* and, at that moment, the fullest and most articulate presentation of Heidegger's *Being and Time* that existed in the French language. Since it was possible to perhaps study with him, under his supervision, I therefore began developing a more intensive interest in Heidegger. I visited De Waelhens before I left Louvain at the end of my theological studies with the intention of returning there. I grew convinced that there were good reasons for continuing to study in Louvain and with De Waelhens.[10]

During that year that followed, the year of Ascetical Theology, which is a form of spiritual formation that the Jesuits required at the end of a formation period, I spend much time reflecting on what precisely it was that I was interested in doing.

Another subject that interested me was the philosophical background of Karl Rahner, a German theologian who had been influenced by Heidegger. So during the summer of that year I visited Karl Rahner and spoke to him about

---

[10] Richardson's reference is to *La Philosophie de Martin Heidegger*, published by Alphonse De Waelhens (1910–1981) in 1942. Professor De Waelhens later developed an interest in psychoanalysis, publishing a book length study on Lacan's interpretation of the psychoses in 1972.

working on some philosophical aspect of his work. I told him that I was interested in the problem of death and he was gracious enough to say: "Here behind me are all my notes on the philosophy and theology of death. If you want them they're all yours. I am too old and too stupid to work on them any further". This was typical of Rahner, a profound and deeply humble man.[11]

At that moment that seemed very attractive but I discovered that Heidegger, who was at Freiburg, was going to teach the following semester, this was in the fall of 1955. I felt that if it were possible to receive permission from the University to do the first term of my graduate studies in philosophy at Freiburg, rather than in Louvain, and with Heidegger himself, that this would be a valid reason for studying Heidegger rather than Karl Rahner. It was an opportunity to see a major figure actually functioning at the height of his form. It was, I think, the last course Heidegger planned to give before fully retiring at Freiburg. The course he was giving then was on the "Principle of Reason."[12]

---

[11] Karl Rahner (1904–1984), considered by many the most important Catholic theologian of the 20th Century, was a German Jesuit. His voluminous publications and writings reveal the influence of diverse theological and philosophical sources, including Thomas Aquinas and Martin Heidegger.

[12] Heidegger, *Der Satz vom Grund*, Heidegger's 1955-1956 lecture course at Freiburg University. Text available as volume 10 to his *Gesamtausgabe*, the official edition of Heidegger's complete works. Published by the Vittorio Klostermann publishing house in Frankfurt am Main, the collection now numbers more than 100 volumes.

The University of Louvain and its Higher Institute of Philosophy gave me permission to spend that first semester in Freiburg and so that's what I did. And so it was by serendipity that I came to study Heidegger. All things being equal, I might well have chosen to study with Karl Rahner, who had been influenced by Heidegger. His *Spirit in the World*, one of his major works, was basically a Heideggerian view of the world as presented in *Being and Time*.[13]

These are some of the reasons for why I decided to work on Heidegger and with Professor De Waelhens who agreed to direct my work if I decided to continue at Louvain.

MB: How interesting. So it was, if I heard correctly, it was because your Jesuit Superiors ordered you to study philosophy that you ended up studying philosophy and ultimately Heidegger. You had at first wanted to study theology?

WJR: Yes. Ordered. That's a harsh word for it, Mario. But that is what they wanted me to do and that's what I signed up for.

MB: I see.

WJR: I would have preferred to study theology but that was not to be.

MB: So let us thank the Jesuits! Your doctoral dissertation on Heidegger was first published in 1963 and under the title "Heidegger: Through Phenomenology to Thought." I have always been

---

[13] Richardson's reference is to Rahner's doctoral dissertation, published in 1939 as *Geist in Welt*.

deeply impressed by that work because, despite the fact that it was written during the early days of Heidegger scholarship, it is still, in my view, the first and only book that really provides a comprehensive, overall understanding of the trajectory of Heidegger's project. You managed this even before Heidegger had passed away. I find that truly amazing and a testimony to the rigor of your work.[14]

How was it that you were able to produce such a manuscript so early on in the history of Heidegger scholarship? How did you manage such a comprehensive view? Was it the help of Heidegger himself?

WJR: Through serendipity, if you wish. I had no idea of what I would work on in Heidegger. I knew that I would have a chance to hear him, possibly to meet him, at least to see him and to work with people who were experienced students of his. I found a place to live in Freiburg. It was in an old people's home and mostly women lived there. I was there as chaplain, and I was succeeding another Jesuit who had been chaplain there the previous year who had finished his work but was still living there during the summer. He had been invited,

---

[14] Richardson, *Heidegger: Through Phenomenology to Thought*, preface by Martin Heidegger (The Hague: Martinus Nijhoff, 1963), a thick tome of 768 pages.

because of his own work on Heidegger, to join a seminar led by Heidegger on *Hegel's Logic*.

I met this man in the summertime and he was to be there the following year and so we spend sometime together. I really got to know him. He was a really enthusiastic person who was very ebullient and loved philosophy and loved to talk.

MB: His name?

WJR: Cannot remember . . . He would attend the seminar, this was in the fall of 1955, and would come back from his meetings with Heidegger and other members of the faculty who had been invited to attend the seminar in Heidegger's home in Freiburg. There were maybe 10, 12 to 15 maximum, who attended the seminar. He came home just full of Heidegger, full of what he said and the interpretations of Hegel. He was the first one to tell me that what De Waelhens had written about Heidegger was now *dépassée*, and that Heidegger would insist upon his actual thought at the time, the academic year of 1955/1956.

So I heard from . . . Virgilio Fagone — I think that was his name, Fagone, who subsequently worked on the staff of the Università Cattolica in Rome. At that time, Fagone had finished his degree and was in Freiburg because he had been invited to take part in the seminar. He was a very, very brilliant guy, like a child exploring his *Brave New World*. So I began to hear about Heidegger from Virgilio. He was very generous and would tell me about what happened that day in the seminar and the differences about an earlier Heidegger as interpreted by De Waelhens and the actual Heidegger who corrected the question of whether Heidegger was an existentialist, which was De Waelhens's assertion.

De Waelhens was basically a phenomenologist. He was a very competent reader of Merleau-Ponty, of *Being and Time* and certainly of Sartre. It was therefore a more Sartrean, or at least a more existentialistic approach to Heidegger than Heidegger would accept. So, from the very beginning, I was introduced to a later Heidegger, one that corrected, if not the earlier Heidegger, the interpretations of Heidegger available at that time.

So it was the fact that I was suddenly in a world where there were at least two periods, or at least two ways of reading Heidegger. One, the French one, which was basically an existentialist interpretation under the leadership of De Waelhens, and the second, a more philosophical and more practical interpretation of Heidegger in terms of the problem of Being as such. So it was in that sense that I began to take note, in my reading, of what Heidegger says when you read him, because there is a difference [between the two periods]. My first impression of Heidegger was of a thinker who had gone through at least two periods, and that none had been maintained until a certain and clear coherence developed in [and between] the two periods. I decided that the most useful way that I could put to use the opportunity that was given me was to try and decide on what to give whom in Heidegger in view of the period one was working on.

I went to see Eugen Fink, who was an assistant of Husserl and had become a student of Heidegger in the late 20's when he first arrived at Freiburg. I spoke to him about the idea of maybe working on a study of Heidegger that would compare Husserl's notion of phenomenology with Heidegger's notion of phenomenology. And Fink said: "No, No. That's too big."[15]

Then I thought about working on the notion of thought in Heidegger. Actually it was Fagone who suggested it to me when he invited me to supper one night. The notion of thought in Heidegger certainly appeared in Heidegger after the late period, so it would be interesting to see if it appeared and how it appeared in the early period. So I noted that as a possible study. That turned out to be decisive. So, I talked with Fink and also with Bernard Welte, who was professor of what they call

---

[15] Eugen Fink (1905–1975) was an associate and aide to Edmund Husserl. He was appointed Husserl's private assistant in 1929 and remained close to Husserl until his death in 1938. Widely recognized as Husserl's best authorized interpreter during his lifetime, Fink began to criticize central aspects of Husserlian phenomenology in the early 1950's, moving closer to Heidegger' s and the latter's "ontological method." Fink co-taught a seminar on Heraclitus with Heidegger during the winter of 1966/1967 whose text Lacan was to highly praise and recommend to his students in 1973. See Lacan's intervention during the Sixth Congress of the Ecole Freudienne de Paris in Grande Motte, near Montpelier, on November 2nd of 1973 (published in volume 15 of the *Lettres de l'Ecole Freudienne de Paris*).

"*Grenzfrage*," a borderline subject between philosophy and Catholic theology.[16]

I also talked to others, such as the assistants of the professors, and asked the question of what they thought would be worthwhile exploring. These assistants were individuals who had already finished their doctorates and were then working on their habilitation theses. So I talked to all of these people as the end of the semester approached.

Heidegger would lecture every Friday, I think it was at five o'clock, and he was giving his course on the "Principle of Reason." I saw that outside of his door there were no lines and I figured: "well, what can I lose? He can't resent my naiveté." He could feel sorry for it or he could dismiss it. But at least, what would I lose if I met the lion at his den, sort of speak. So I screwed on my courage to go speak to him and decided to go in and see him with my broken German.

And he was very gracious to me. He could have just dismissed me but didn't. He really treated me like a *Mensch*, so to speak. I told him what I was interested in doing and that I was interested in working on his work. I told him then that three things appealed to me as a student [of his] and that I would be grateful if he would just react [to them].

One was a comparison of his conception of phenomenology and that of Husserl. I told him that

---

[16] Bernhard Welte (1906–1983) was a Jesuit priest and religious philosopher who was appointed to the philosophy chair in Christian Religion at Freiburg University in 1954

Professor Fink suggested that that would be too large. And he said: "Oh yeah, that's much too large." I also told him that I was interested in his essay "The Essence of Ground," where he speaks of the ontological difference, and asked him whether he had written anything else on the ontological difference.[17]

He sort of rolled his eyes. All of the later work, for probably the last ten years, was around the notion of the ontological difference. And he said that yes, he had written other things that had not been published in that area. So, I said, "then we better wait until they are published." "Yeah, I think so." he said.

MB: And the third topic was...?

WJR: was the question of Thought [*Denken*]. I found traces of the notion of thought from *Being and Time* through the later work as I worked to find out what he meant by it. And he said: "Yes!" So I said: "Do you think that is really feasible?" And he said: "Yeah." And so I went and told De Waelhens of my conversation with Heidegger

MB: and he said...?

WJR: He looked at me as if I was out of my mind and said: "Are you serious?" And I said: "Yes!" He also said that the later Heidegger was no longer philosophy but just poetry. In his own work he had established his reputation by articulating his

---

[17] Richardson is apparently referring to *Vom Wesens des Grundes* written in 1928 and published by Heidegger a year later as a contribution to a *Festschrift* for Edmund Husserl. The essay is available in volume 9 of the Gesammtausgabe.

conception of Heidegger's philosophy based on the earlier period and I was interested in doing something that related to the later period, which for him was just sheer poetry. So he fell deep in thought and shook his head and said: "Well, it's your decision. Are you really serious? Do you realize what you're saying?" And I was, of course, going by what Heidegger said, so it wasn't my word against De Waelhens it was Heidegger against De Waelhens about Heidegger. "Yes, that's what I would like to work on!"

And he again shook his head and said: "Well, good luck. I'll try to direct you the best way I can but I have to tell you now that I don't think it's a viable subject." And I came to realize later that maybe he saw, better than I did, well I don't think he did, I think he really believed that the later Heidegger was just poetry and no longer philosophy.

It was only when I began to give him chapters to read that he saw the value of the research. By the time I had finished the earlier period, leading up through 1929, and saw that what I was doing was really headed in a direction that completely sabotaged his reading [of Heidegger].

To his credit, De Waelhens never mentioned the fact. He was supportive and encouraged me all the time and gave me very carefully analysed reactions to my chapters with rigor and courtesy and kindness. Again, he did this despite the fact that he saw, better than I did, that I was really sabotaging his position. There was a decisive moment in Heidegger's development when Heidegger himself realized that the subject of *Being and Time* did not and could not work.

Eventually, I did not realize this until much latter, I saw that what I was doing was really undercutting the entire conception that De Waelhens had. And to his credit, he honored his task of being a critic and a patron and saw the value of the work.

As a matter of fact at one point, after I had finished the so call early period up until 1929, I was getting tired and just wanted to get back to the [United] States to teach and to just finish what had to be done from home. He told me at that point that I had sufficient work for a doctoral thesis and that all I had to do was to give him a month to process it. "But," he said, "you have developed a method that is satisfactory from my point of view. The earlier period has been worked through. You have worked through it and you have come up with something different. The earlier essays have been discussed, but now it is time for the later period."

He added that if I really wanted to do something that would be a real contribution then I should keep using the same method and continue on to the later period to at least clarify what happened, how the notion of thought developed and so on.

MB: On the question of thought, I now see more clearly how it is that you have come from Heidegger and the question of thought in Heidegger to Freud. Having read most of your published work, it now seems to me that what ties together your movement from Heidegger to psychoanalysis is the problem or question of thought. It's interesting that in your Heidegger book you decided to not treat the question of theology, the question of God in Heidegger. Not because there is nothing to say but rather, as you mention early on in the text, because there was in fact so much to say. You had wanted to study theology but yet the question of God was not treated there. I am in fact recalling your having quoted a few lines from a poem by Dylan Thomas, "Vision and Prayer," in your Heidegger book and that you decided to leave out the words "and prayer" from the title, citing it as "Vision . . .," with an ellipsis in place of the words "and Prayer."

Later on in your career you of course did broach the question of theology in Heidegger as well as the God question as it relates to Freud and psychoanalysis in light of Lacan.[18] Sara, would you like to pose a question?

SH: Perhaps we ought to start addressing the question of psychoanalysis. Maybe it can be done through the question of thought.

MB: I agree. What are we to make of your passage from Heideggerian thought to psychoanalytic thought, and in particularly the question of the

---

[18] Richardson has addressed the God question in Heidegger and in psychoanalysis in a number of essays, including "Heidegger and God — and Professor Jonas," *Thought*, 40: 13-40 (1965); "Psychoanalysis and the God-Question" in Thought," 61: (1986): 68-83; and "'Like Straw': Religion and Psychoanalysis" in *Eros and Eris: Contributions to a Hermeneutic Phenomenology* (The Hague: Kluwer Academic Publishers, 1992), pp, 93-104.

unconscious? The question of the unconscious is one that has preoccupied you for the last quarter century.

WJR: I traced the first mention of thought, as distinct from phenomenology, as something that began to be given [in Heidegger] in 1930. It was not published until 1943. During this time the change that took place in Heidegger, whatever it was, was called "the Turn." Heidegger's word is *"Kehre."* It involves a turn from the phenomenology that De Waelhens had developed to this notion of thought or the thinking of Being which characterized the later period in Heidegger.

That change, as I've said, took place between 1930 and 1943 and it could be depicted in this one essay called "On the Essence of Truth." Given the various forms of redaction there was no way for me to know what changes had been made between the 1930 text and the 1943 text finally published. All I had was the published text that was available. There were no pirated editions floating around, or at least not available to me. So I decided at that point that I would restrict myself to what had been published rather than trying to check out all possible manuscripts of the essay.[19]

---

[19] Heidegger, „Vom Wesen der Wahrheit," lecture pronounced by Heidegger in 1930 (Bremen). Heidegger apparently revised the text several times, delivering it on various occasions, under the same name title and in different cities, during the next few years. The essay was first published in 1943. The final version of the text may be found in volume 9 of the *Gesamtausgabe*. Heidegger's 1930 lecture is not to be confused with *Vom Wesen der Wahrheit. Zu Platon's Hohlengleichnis und Theatet*, his winter semester

There was no talk at that time of Heidegger publishing all his unpublished texts. In fact, when I met with him in 1959, he pointed behind him to an entire bookcase filled with the courses he had given. He said something like: "people want me to publish all that stuff. I can do that when I am an old man," he said, "right now I feel fresh and I'll just move forward."

So there was no thought in anyone's mind, as far as I knew, and as far as the cognoscenti knew, of it ever being published. So I figured it was a good risk to limit myself to what had been published at that time. I began reading the essay "On the Essence of Truth" and worked through everything chronologically that had been published, or was available or was soon to be published.

Heidegger had been suspended from the University in 1945 because of his involvement with the Nazi's. He gave a course in 1952 after having been denazified or having gone through the denazification process.[20]

So in 1952 he returned to teaching after having been suspended since 1945. The course he gave in 1952 was called *Was heißt Denken?* or "What is called or meant by thinking" or "thought" And there was all of the ambiguity about the calling.

---

course at Freiburg University in 1931-1932 which has been published as volume 34 of his *Gesamtausgabe*.

[20] For Richardson's position on Heidegger's involvement with the Nazi's, see his "Heidegger's Fall" in Babich, ed., *From Phenomenology to Thought. Essays in Honor of William J. Richardson S.J.* (Dordrecht: Kluwer, 1995), pp. 619-629.

"Who does the calling?" "What is the calling?" And so forth . . .²¹

Anyway, I eventually had a manuscript of around 1,100 pages containing about 5000 notes so I figured I had to stop sometime and to limit myself to what was explicitly contained there.

When I came home to the States I had therefore already met Heidegger. I was actually introduced to Heidegger by Professor Max Müller. Max Müller had become a good friend of Virgilio Fagone and he in turn introduced me to Max Müller. Max Müller became a sort of second mentor to the dissertation. Anyway, it was Max Müller who helped me to meet with Heidegger. He wrote him a letter of introduction telling him about my work and that it was worth paying attention to.²²

So through the good offices of Max Müller, just before I began to edit the text for presentation of the doctorate, in the spring of 1960, I [again] went to see Heidegger. He apparently liked my work and responded favorably to it. I had sent him a summary of twenty-five pages of my large manuscript. He pulled it out of his [desk] drawer and I saw that it was marked red and blue, like an American flag, every page, and with circles around

---

[21] Heidegger, *Was heißt Denken?* (*What is Called Thinking?*). Composed by Heidegger between 1951 and 1952 and first delivered by him during the 1952 summer semester. Its text was first published in Germany two years later, in 1954, and can be found in volume 8 of the *Gesamtausgabe*.

[22] Max Müller (1906–1994) was a philosopher and disciple of Heidegger who taught at Freiburg University.

it. And I immediately thought "good Lord. Here we go."
He accepted it and actually only made two suggestions, both of which I considered minor. Firstly, he said that I had used the word *Subjectivität*, and that that pertained to Descartes. He said that when you talk about Leibniz, in the German tradition, the word should no longer be *Subjectivität* but *Subjektität*. So it is no longer subjectivity but subject-ness. At least that's what I understood at the time. That was the only serious criticism he had, which was fair enough. I was grateful to him and glad that there was nothing more serious than that.
At any rate, by reason of his suggestions I presented my dissertation defense as soon as possible, at the end of the exam period in the spring of 1960. I was then invited to do what they call in Louvain the *"aggrégation."* It was a way of becoming an honorary member of the Faculty. It required a publication of a book such as the *"Habilitationsschrift."* So it was a sort of second degree or second level of a doctorate. That was by invitation only and it was by the invitation of the faculty. At any rate, I was invited to the aggregation, called at that time *aggregé,* and was committed to come back and finish up the *"aggrégation."*
The next two years were basically devoted to preparing the aggregation and to editing the text. I presented the first part of it alone as my doctoral

thesis and then the second part became the book as I began expansion of the thesis into the book.

When I came home, having finished the book and the book having been published, or about to be published, I began to be interrogated about the relevance of Heidegger. I was questioned, in particular, by the members of the world of what was then called "Existential Psychoanalysis." Rollo May and Leslie Farber were the two major figures in America at that time. They asked me to explain what Heidegger meant by his work.[23]

Rollo had done work on Binswanger, a big presentation on existential psychoanalysis. Binswanger, for all intent and purposes, introduced the notion of Dasein into the field of psychiatry and psychology and developed a form of psychotherapy that was basically Husserlian. His formation was largely in Husserl. He was a fine and admirable person and his work was fine work but based on the phenomenology of Husserl.[24]

---

[23] Rollo May (1909–1994) was an American psychologist and psychoanalyst who stood as the leading spokesman for an existential and phenomenological interpretation of Freudian psychoanalysis during the decade of the 50's and 60's. Leslie H. Farber, who died in 1981, was an American psychologist. He was a former Chairman of the Washington D.C. School of Psychiatry and a Director of Therapy at the Austen Riggs Center in Massachusetts. His book *The Ways of the Will*, published in 1966, was highly praised, including by members of the American and International psychoanalytic community.

[24] Ludwig Binswanger (1881–1966) came from a Jewish family in Osterberg (Bavaria). He served, for 45 years, as medical director of the Bellevue sanitarium, a famous psychiatric hospital in Kreuzlingen (Switzerland) founded by his grandfather.

Rollo May had published his own book based on Binswanger by then and asked me to join a seminar dealing with Heidegger. I did and that got me involved with the field of scholars dealing with existential psychoanalysis.[25]

Then I was asked to teach seminarians. This was in 1963 when the seminarians and students all over the United States were caught up in the sweep leading up to 1968 and that exploded in America in '68, in Berkeley. But 1963 was the year that [John

---

    Binswanger studied under Jung and Bleuler at the Zurich Burgholzli in 1907 and, in March of that year, accompanied Jung in his famous visit to Vienna to meet with Freud. Freud and Binswanger became and remained lifelong friends following their 1907 meeting. On this point, see the 1992 publication of the Freud-Binswanger correspondence. Binswanger is considered the father of *Daseinanalyse*, a term he adopted in the 1940's. His efforts to ground psychiatry within a phenomenological anthropological framework reveals the influence of both Husserlian and Heideggerian philosophy. Heidegger was to openly disagree with Binswanger's interpretation of his philosophy and Binswanger in turn spoke of his "productive misunderstanding" of Heidegger. The influence of Husserl, as Richardson suggests, was indeed more prevalent in the case of Binswanger. This held especially true during the first and last periods of Binswanger's production. The depth of the theoretical impact of Freud on Binswanger, despite the fact that Binswanger had served as President of the Zurich Psychoanalytic Society in 1910 and that he claimed being unable to "manage without the unconscious," either in his "psychotherapeutic practice" or "in theory," remains a matter difficult to assess.

[25] Richardson's reference is to *Existence: A New Dimension in Psychiatry and Psychology* (New York: Basic Books, 1958), the first book to provide English language readers with access to a representative selection of the work of European thinkers in the area of "Existential Psychoanalysis." Rollo May served as the main editor of the project. The book featured the work of Binswanger in particular.

F.] Kennedy was shot, shortly after that [in 1968] Martin Luther King was killed. The Beatles came to America then [in 1964] and Bob Dylan began to sing. This was the world in which I was asked to teach.

The seminarians were of course part of that world and they felt the restlessness of the time. I had a good Jesuit friend who was an enormously intelligent man and a very wise man but his health made it impossible to be an academic, to go through graduate studies, and he was the spiritual father of the seminarians. I was sent there extensively to do research but was told upon arrival that they had just lost two professors and I was their only replacement. So I was committed and caught up in teaching.

And I got along with the students. To this day some of my closest friends were my students who were troubled late teenagers or in their early twenties then and who were feeling the pulse of their times with lots of early 20 problems.

MB: And you were teaching them what?

WJR: I was teaching them philosophy. I was told that I was the replacement for the professor in the history of philosophy and for the professor that taught them natural theology as well.

MB: When exactly did you turn to Freud?

WJR: Late in the sixties. I had to devote time counseling students. It was very weary physically. I was helping them deal with their academic problems and was using a mixture of psychotherapy with theology. So I decided, in 1970, that if I could be accepted for psychoanalytic training, it would be helpful. I then went to the William Alanson White Institute in New York for my training. I made all the necessary moves and cut all ties to philosophy.[26]

I later went to work at Austen Riggs in Massachusetts, just north of New York.[27]

At the end of 1974-1975 [while at Austen Riggs] I was introduced to the name of Lacan. It was by Ed Podvoll, the grandson of a surgeon who had studied medicine at Columbia [University]. Podvoll had spent 10 years at Chestnut Lodge and was intrigued by the difficulties of Lacan and the practical implications and the application of Lacan.[28]

In the meantime, a former student of mine, John Muller, came aboard [at Austen Riggs]. He was a child of the sixties and had spent three years at an Indian reservation. He had been interested in

---

[26] The William Alanson White Institute of Psychiatry, Psychoanalysis and Psychology, from which Richardson graduated in 1974, was founded in New York City in 1946 by Clara Thompson, Harry Stack Sullivan and Erich Fromm. Denied acceptance into the American Psychoanalytic Association soon after its founding because it allowed psychologists to receive psychoanalytic training, it operates today as an independent psychoanalytic institute in the same city.

[27] The Austen Riggs Center is a small open psychiatric hospital in Stockbridge (Massachusetts). It has retained a strong psychoanalytic orientation since it was founded in 1919.

[28] Chestnut Lodge is a psychiatric hospital in Rockville (Maryland). Founded in 1910, it has a long tradition of offering intensive and psychoanalytically based treatment to individuals diagnosed with psychosis and other serious mental disorders.

Indian folklore and Indian imagery and was even made an honorary Indian, of all things.[29]

MB: What year was this?

WJR: This was 1975. That's when I began to hear about Lacan, this "impossible man." I was told "Lacan is a big name. He is impossible to understand but he is the big name."

But let me finish with Podvoll, who first introduced me to Lacan. He was so enthusiastic about Lacan that right now I would be suspicious of him. This was the end of 1974, start of 1975. He, as director of education [at Austen Riggs], had the freedom to decide on how the fellows — these were all post doctoral students, post graduate people in psychiatry and psychology — should train during their four years of research and clinical work.[30] Ed

---

[29] John P. Muller received his doctorate in psychology from Harvard University and is a graduate of the Boston Psychoanalytic Institute. Muller is the author of *Beyond the Psychoanalytic Dyad. Developmental Semiotics in Freud, Pierce and Lacan* (New York: Routledge, 1996). He has been associated with the Austen Riggs Center for a number of years and is today its Director of Training. Along with Richardson, Muller was a founding member of the Lacan Clinical Forum at Austen Riggs.

[30] Edward M. Podvoll was born in 1936 and graduated from New York University Medical School. He trained as a psychiatrist at Bellevue Hospital in New York and was a graduate of the Washington Psychoanalytic Institute where he also served as a faculty member. A former staff member of Chestnut Lodge Hospital and a Director of Training and Education at the Austen Riggs Center, Dr. Podvoll later became a Buddhist monk and directed the "contemplative psychotherapy department" at the East-West psychology program at Naropa University in Boulder (Colorado). Podvoll went on to found the "Windhorse Project" in Boulder as a result of his meditative experiences. Offering a new framework of treatment to individuals suffering from psychosis,

Podvoll was so convinced [about Lacan] that he wanted to rearrange the entire training program at Austen Riggs. This was in 1975. Austen Riggs was a place that was traditionally ego psychology. David Rapaport and Erik Erikson were the two chief figures there. Anyway, Podvoll became more and more extreme in his lifetime. So much so that he set up this entire program for training the fellows and, by the time we began to teach it, just before the academic year began, Ed Podvoll got involved with a former patient, which was forbidden, and he was dismissed.

So there we were, John and I, stuck, so to speak, with a new training program for the fellows, although we knew nothing, basically, about Lacan. John knew less than I. Anyway, that's how it began for us. I was also committed to teach graduate courses at Fordham University in New York. So John and I began to co-teach a course on the

---

its model of care is based largely on Buddhist principles and on insights developed by Podvoll in his book *The Seductions of Madness: Revolutionary Insights into the World of Psychosis and a Compassionate Approach to Recovery at Home*, published by Harper Collins in 1990. Podvoll left for Europe soon after the publication of his book, completing an 11-year meditative retreat in a Buddhist monastery in France before returning to the United States and to Colorado in 2002. An updated and expanded edition of his book was reissued by Shambhala Publication in 2003 under a new title *Recovering Sanity: A Comprehensive Approach to Understanding and Treating Psychosis*. Described by its new publisher as "an underground classic," the book received highly positive reviews, including from members of the American psychoanalytic establishment. Dr Podvoll died of cancer in Boulder (Colorado) in December of 2003, at the age of 67.

"function and field of speech and language in psychoanalysis."[31]

MB: So, how were you able to begin to think of the work of Lacan in light of your past training in theology and Heidegger? Was there a clash? An epiphany? or experience?

SH: This might perhaps be the last question because I would also like to ask a question about the current situation in psychoanalysis in the United States.

MB: Well, perhaps one or two additional questions. This material seems interesting and important, at least to me.

WJR: John and I began to teach together. We would prepare our courses together for both Fordham University and for the fellows [at Austen Riggs]. And it was in this way that we went through those essays of the *Ecrits* that were then published.[32]

---

[31] American intellectuals were first exposed to the work of Lacan precisely through this essay, his now famous 1953 Rome Discourse, which appeared in English language translation by Anthony Wilden, with extensive notes and commentary by him, in 1968. See *The Language of the Self* (Baltimore: John Hopkins University Press, 1968). Lacan's text reveals strong traces of the influence of Heidegger, particularly when he argues on behalf of the symbolic constitution of human subjectivity.

[32] Nine of the essays found in Lacan's *Ecrits* were published in English translation (by Alan Sheridan) in 1977. The essays chosen for translation and publication then stood as a partial selection of the twenty-nine major texts and six introductions and appendices which make up the entire text of the *Ecrits*, published in 1966. The first complete English language translation of Lacan's *Ecrits* is scheduled to appear through W.W. Norton & Company in January of 2006, translation by Bruce Fink.

MB: In 1977.

WJR: Yes. And at the same time we got to know Claudia, one of Lacan's former students and analysands, who had learned about our work. So we met with Claudia and began to think that if we wanted to really do this what we ought to do is go through a Lacanian analysis. So this brings us up to 1978. Lacan, around that time, came to America to give a series of lectures.[33] Podvoll and I, this was just before John Muller arrived at Austen Riggs, went down to hear him at Yale [University]. Podvoll was completely enthusiastic. At the end of the lecture, which had started with the Law School auditorium filled with 500 people and was left, at the end of an hour, with about 25, including Podvoll and myself, I turned to Ed and asked: "Well, what do you think Ed?" And he answered: "Well, the man is either a genius, or a charlatan or he is mad." That was Podvoll's impression of Lacan's lecture.

But by this time we were committed to teaching Lacan. It was soon after that that Ed left us and that John came aboard. So we had to make do and to prepare introductory courses on Lacan's *Ecrits*. And we decided that if we wanted to continue this

---

[33] Richardson's reference is to a series of lectures Lacan delivered in some of the more important universities in the American northeast in the winter of 1975. Lacan spoke at Yale University in New Haven (Connecticut) on November 24 (Kanzer Seminar) and November 25 (Law School Auditorium). He also lectured at Columbia University in New York City a few days later, on December 1st, and at the Massachusetts Institute of Technology in Boston on December 2nd. See « Conférences et entretiens dans les universités nord-américaines, » *Scilicet*, vol. 6/7 (1975): 7-45.

we would have to get ourselves analyzed [by a Lacanian] so we could give it a go.

In that year there was a *Petites Journées* on transmission, maybe some remember, and Claudia was there. She came and introduced us to Lacan, although I had already met him on a previous occasion. So she arrived at the *Journées*, at the opening session, and we came over to her when we saw her. She introduced us to Lacan and told him that we would like to meet [with] him. And he said: "OK, Monday morning at 11 o'clock." This was now Friday evening and we said that we would be there. He came [to the meeting] wearing a bathrobe and in his slippers.

MB: This was at his house?

WJR: Yes, which was also his office. And he came in and said: "*Allô, de quoi s'agit il?*" So we told him and he said: "OK, come back Thursday at 1." So that was it. John was with his wife and he had planned to travel with her and she was already unhappy with the idea of spending time away from traveling. I was planning to travel to Rome. John and I both changed our plans to have lunch with Lacan. Silvia was there and we also met Judith, his daughter. Jacques-Alain Miller was supposed to have been there and Lacan himself. So we had a private lunch with Lacan. He offered us a shot of Jack Daniels during lunch. It was very gracious and very generous of him.

It was at that point that I was invited to lecture at Oxford [University] the following year, in the fall of [19]79.[34]

I decided that this was my chance, you know. I had to break obligations with patients. So I was scheduled to lecture in Oxford and to also come to Paris and thus had a year and a half off before going back to teaching in the [United] States. This was around the time that the Ecole Freudienne de Paris collapsed, so that was my second exposure to Lacan.

But by this time, because of the involvement with John, we decided that we could make a book out of the collaboration we had done on the 9 essays of the *Ecrits*, which we did. Our book has since been translated into French.[35]

So by that time I was into Lacan. I did not get into analysis with Lacan but with someone whom Lacan did not suggest but of whom he did approve. After this I returned to America and to teaching and to seeing patients and so on.

SH: Who, then, was Heidegger for Lacan?

WJR: Heidegger was for Lacan an important person. He published in 1956, in *La Psychanalyse*, a very good translation of Heidegger's *Logos* essay.

---

[34] Professor Richardson served as Martin D'Arcy Lecturer at Oxford University in England in 1979.

[35] Besides *Lacan and Language: A Reader's Guide to the Ecrits* (New York: International Universities Press, 1982), Muller and Richardson's collaborative efforts also include *The Purloined Poe: Lacan, Derrida, and Psychoanalytic Reading* (Baltimore: John Hopkins University Press, 1988).

The essay of course deals with the notion of language, that is, the late Heidegger.[36]

Jean Beaufret had published "On Humanism" and was a patient that Lacan took into psychoanalysis. Lacan found Heidegger's notion of "speaking language" very appealing and used Heidegger as a propaedeutic; he says so [early on] in *Seminar XI*, which took place in late 1963 and in 1964. Heidegger himself, however, was not sympathetic to psychoanalysis.[37] In 1964, Lacan got into topology and went his way alone. In 1959 he worked on *das Ding* or *La Chose*.[38]

---

[36] See Martin Heidegger, "Logos (Heraclit, Fragment 50)," translated by Jacques Lacan, *La Psychanalyse*, Vol. I (1956): 59-79.

[37] Heidegger's "Letter on 'Humanism'" was a letter Heidegger penned to Jean Beaufret in Paris in the Fall of 1946 in response to a communication from the French philosopher which, among other things, asked Heidegger: "Comment redonner un sens au mot 'Humanisme?'" [How can we restore meaning to the word 'humanism']. The text of Heidegger's response to Beaufret was first published in 1947 and can be found in volume 9 of the *Gesamtausgabe*. Heidegger's dictum "die Sprache spricht" [Language speaks] can be found in his October 7, 1950 lecture "Die Sprache" [Language], volume 12 of the *Gesamtausgabe*. A related thesis, Heidegger's "Language is the House of Being," appears in his "Letter on 'Humanism.'"

[38] Heidegger, *Das Ding* [The Thing] was first presented by Heidegger in the form of a lecture at the Bayerischen Akademie der Schönen Kunste on June 6, 1950. The text of Heidegger's presentation was published a year later and is today found in volume 7 of his *Gesamtausgabe* (pp. 163-181). Lacan made heavy use of Heidegger's essay in his seminar on the ethics of psychoanalysis (1959-1960). Leaning on Heidegger's phenomenological analysis of *Das Ding*, Lacan labored to provide Freud's use of the concept with a new twist, retrieving it as central for psychoanalytic theory in the process. Consult Lacan's

lectures of December 16, 1959 and January 27 of 1960 in particular. Like Heidegger, Lacan was to appeal to the fact that the French word for Thing [*Chose*] derived from the Latin "Causa," a link which seems to have determined the title he selected for his November 7, 1955 lecture in Vienna "La chose freudienne ou Sens de retour à Freud en psychanalyse," later included for publication in his *Ecrits*. Lacan was to return to Heidegger's essay and to the German philosopher's celebrated analysis of a pitcher or vase as "Thing" found therein in the penultimate lecture of his 9th seminar in Paris. In it, we find Lacan calling on Heidegger's doctrine of "Geviert" [Four Fold] to treat the question of space [*latum, longum et profundum*], categories alone open to *Dasein*, the Shepard of Being. All of this obviously hints at the importance of Heidegger for grasping the philosophical underpinnings of Lacan's return to Freud, including his very conception of psychoanalytic treatment. The very title to Lacan's 1958 presentation at Royaumont on the "direction of the cure" [*la direction de la cure*] serves to betray the influence of Heidegger over him. For here we find Lacan appealing to the term "cure" rather than "traitement" (he had invoked the latter term to provide his essay on the possible "treatment" of psychosis with its name) and as he furnishes the principal text where he was to detail his conception and vision of psychoanalytic care with its title. Lacan's use of the word "cure" rather than "*traitement*" appears to harken back to Heidegger's *Being and Time*, to section 42 of the text in particular, wherein the German thinker had called on the little-known but influential Graeco-Roman myth of *Cura* to describe the basic structure of man, *Dasein*, as *Sorge* [Care]. The influence of Heidegger seems present throughout the entire essay, including its last paragraph where we find Lacan reflecting on "the final *Spaltung* [splitting] by which the subject is linked to the Logos, and about which Freud was beginning to write, giving us, at the final point of an oeuvre that has the dimension of [B]eing, the solution to `infinite' analysis, when his death applied to it the word `Nothing'." Logos and Being are of course terms associated with Heidegger. The same holds true for the word 'Nothing' when capitalized. For let us recall the fact that it had been precisely in his essay on *Das Ding* that Heidegger, for the first time, began to describe death as "the shrine of Nothing, that is, of that which in every respect

MB: Did you think Heidegger understood the unconscious?

WJR: Heidegger was not sympathetic to Lacan's understanding of the unconscious. He did not know much about Freud. He did work on clinical cases and had some [idea of] clinical experience. His knowledge [in this area] came mainly from Medard Boss. The relationship between Boss and Heidegger became a friendship, rare in that age.[39]

Boss found Heidegger's analysis of Dasein very attractive. He got to know Heidegger's thought around 1940 and they began to take trips together after they got to know each other. Heidegger was near St. Moritz and regularly traveled to Switzerland to teach there at Boss's request.[40]

---

is never something that merely exists, but which nevertheless presences, even as the mystery of Being itself."

[39] Medard Boss (1903–1990) was a Swiss psychiatrist who founded the daseinsanalytic method of psychotherapy. He received psychiatric training at the Zurich Burgholzli under [Eugen] Bleuler and also studied with Carl Jung for a ten-year period. Boss had a number of psychoanalytic sessions with Freud in 1925 and went on to analyze with Karen Horney in Berlin. He received clinical supervision by Hans Sachs, Otto Fenichel and Ernest Jones, among others. Boss appears to have first learned of Heidegger through Binswanger and established contact with the German philosopher soon after, in 1947. The two men quickly became friends and began vacationing together, traveling to Greece in 1962.

[40] Richardson's reference is to Heidegger's Zollikon seminars, a series of lectures Heidegger delivered between 1959 and 1969, at Boss's invitation, before psychiatrist in Zollikon (Switzerland). The text and protocols of these lectures was first published in Germany in 1987 under the title *Zollikoner Seminaire, Protokolle – Gesprache – Briefe Herausgegeben von Medard Boss* (Frankfurt am Main: Vittorio Klostermann). The seminar reveals Heidegger

As for Heidegger's understanding of Freud, it was pathetical. Heidegger criticized Freud's inability to pose the term of possibility, he felt that Freud had failed to understand what Being or "to be" meant. Heidegger, of course, can't account for certain phenomena related to the unconscious.[41]

MB: Obviously — Sara had wanted to pose a question about the status and future of psychoanalysis in the United States.

SH: Yes, how do you see psychoanalysis in your country? What is the current situation and what do you see as its future there?

---

criticizing Freudian metapsychology in general and Freud's view of the unconscious in particular. Boss himself had already claimed in his 1957 book *Psychoanalyse und Daseinsanalytik* that the Daseinsanalytic approach to treatment had no need for the Freudian unconscious. Richardson has offered a powerful response to the daseinanalytic critique of the Freudian unconscious in light of Lacan in his essay "Heidegger among the Doctors," in, John Sallis, ed., *Reading Heidegger: Commemorations* (Bloomington: Indiana University Press, 1983), pp. 49-63.

[41] Richardson has attempted to account for the phenomenon of the unconscious in view of Heideggerian philosophy in his classic and important essay "The Place of the Unconscious in Heidegger" in *Review of Existential Psychology and Psychiatry*, volume 5(3): 265-290 (1965). For an essay which treats the question of what Heidegger could have been to Lacan, and what Heideggerian philosophy can offer Lacanianism, see Richardson's "Truth and Freedom in Psychoanalysis" in Roger Frie, ed., *Understanding Experience: Psychotherapy and Modernism* (London: Routledge, 2003), pp. 77-99. Professor Richardson is currently engaged in researching and evaluating Lacan's formulations on the ethics of psychoanalysis, a project he hopes to publish in the near future.

WJR: Psychoanalysis is moribund and has lost its hold on the American audience. While the work of Lacan appears as a possible source of new life for it, the fact remains that Lacanianism has not caught on with the American psychoanalytic community. It has had and continues to have an impact in our Universities, in the field of literature and literary studies in particular. Lacan's return to Freud as such remains an open question in the United States.

Bill Richardson, Meßkirch, St Martins Friedhof, 2015

WILLIAM J. RICHARDSON, S.J., BIBLIOGRAPHY

BIBLIOGRAPHY OF PUBLISHED WORKS[42]

WILLIAM J. RICHARDSON S.J., Ph.D.
(1 November 1920 – 10 December 2016)

1962

Richardson, William J. (1962a) "Heidegger and the Origin of Language," *International Philosophical Quarterly*, 2: 404-416.

Richardson, William J. (1962b) "Heidegger and the Problem of Thought," *Revue Philosophique de Louvain*, LX: 58-78.

1963

Richardson, William J. (1963a) "Heidegger and Plato," *The Heythrop Journal*, 4: 273-279.

Richardson, William J. (1963b) *Heidegger: Through Phenomenology to Thought*. Preface by Martin Heidegger. The Hague: Nijhoff.

---

[42] Bibliography compiled by Mario Beira. The current editor has added formatting, corrections, some new entries, and located page ranges where possible. Any additional material or corrections would be welcomed.

1964

Richardson, William J. (1964) "Heidegger and Aristotle," *The Heythrop Journal*, 5: 58-64.

1965

Richardson, William J. (1965a) "Heidegger and Theology," *Theological Studies*, 26: 86-100.

Richardson, William J. (1965b) "Heidegger and God — and Professor Jonas," *Thought*, 40:13-40.

Richardson, William J. (1965c) „Heideggers Weg durch die Phänomenologie zum Seinsdenken," *Philosophisches Jahrbuch*, LXII: 385-396 (Original text, written in English, published in 1981).

Richardson, William J. (1965d) "The Place of the Unconscious in Heidegger," *Review of Existential Psychology and Psychiatry*, 5(3): 265-290.

1967

Richardson, William J. (1967a) "Heidegger and the Quest of Freedom," *Theological Studies*, 28: 286-307.

Richardson, William J. (1967b) "Kant and the Late Heidegger," in: J.M. Edie, ed., *Phenomenology in America*, Chicago: Quadrangle, pp. 125-144.

Richardson, William J. (1967c) "Pay any Price? Break any Mold?: The Competence of the Catholic University," *America*, CXVI (April 29), 624-642, reprinted in; N.G. McCluskey S.J., ed., *The Catholic University: A Modern Appraisal*, Notre Dame, Indiana: The University of Notre Dame Press, (1970), pp. 271-290.

1968

Richardson, William J. (1968a) "Heidegger's Critique of Science," *The New Scholasticism*, LXII: 511-536.

Richardson, William J. (1968b) "A Letter from Heidegger: Translation and Commentary," in: Manfred Frings, ed., *Heidegger and the Quest for Truth*, Chicago: Quadrangle Books, pp. 17-27.

Richardson, William J. (1968c) "The Transcendence of God in the World of Man," *Proceedings of the Catholic Theological Society of America*, XXIII: 201-220.

1970

Richardson, William J. (1970a) "The University and Christian Formation," in: N.G. McCluskey, S.J., ed., *The Catholic University: A Modern Appraisal*, St Louis: B. Herder, pp. 157-196

Richardson, William J. (1970b) "The Distinctiveness of Jesuit Higher Education," in E. Grollmes, S.J., ed., *Catholic Colleges and the Secular Mystique*, St Louis: B. Herder, pp. 148-179.

1971

Richardson, William J. (1971a) "Humanism and Existential Psychology," in: T.C. Greening, ed., *Existential Humanistic Psychology*, Belmont, California: Brooks-Cole, pp. 121-133.

Richardson, William J. (1971b) "A Christian View of Progress," *Thought: Fordham University Quarterly*, 46 (4): 562-576.

1976

Richardson, William J. (1976a) "Discussion of H.C. Shands M.D, *Myth or Mental Illness: On the Function of Consensus,*" *Contemporary Psychoanalysis,* 12: 75-81.

Richardson, William J. (1976b) "Personal Human Development," in: W.C. Bier, S.J., ed., *Human Life: Problems of Birth, of Living, of Dying,* New York: Fordham University Press.

1977

Richardson, William J. (1977a) "Martin Heidegger: In Memoriam," *Commonweal,* CIV (7 January 1977), pp. 16-18; reprinted in *Man and World,* Vol. X: 6-12.

Richardson, William J. (1977b) "Heidegger's Way through Phenomenology to the Thinking of Being," *Listening,* XII: 21-37 (first published in German translation in 1965).

1978

Richardson, William J. (1978) "Religion and Mental Health," *Encyclopedia of Bioethics,* Center of Bioethics, Kennedy Institute, Georgetown University, Washington, DC. New York: McMillan, pp. 1064-1071.

Richardson, William J. and John P. Muller (1978) "Toward Reading Lacan: Pages for a Workbook: Chapter 1: The Mirror Stage as Formative of the Function of the I as Revealed in Psychoanalytic Experience," *Psychoanalysis and Contemporary Thought,* 1(3): 355-372.

1978-1979

Richardson, William J. (1978-79) "The Mirror Inside: Problem of the Self," *Review of Existential Psychology and Psychiatry*, Vol. XVI: 95-112.

1980

Richardson, William J. (1980a) "Piaget, Lacan and Language," in: Hugh Silverman, ed., *Piaget: Philosophy and the Human Sciences*, New Jersey: Humanities Press, pp. 144-170.

Richardson, William J. (1980b) "Phenomenology and Psychoanalysis," *Journal of Phenomenological Psychology*, 11 (2): 1-20.

1981

Richardson, William J. (1981) "Heidegger's Way through Phenomenology to the Thinking of Being," in: Thomas Sheehan, ed., *Heidegger: The Man and the Thinker*, Chicago: Precedent Publishing, pp. 79-94.

1982

Richardson, William J. (1982a) "Lacan's View of Language and Being," *The Psychoanalytic Review*, 69: 229-233.

Richardson, William J. and John P. Muller (1982) *Lacan and Language: A Reader's Guide to the Ecrits*. New York: International Universities.

1983

Richardson, William J. (1983a) "Lacan and the Subject of Psychoanalysis" in: Joseph H. Smith and William Kerrigan, eds., *Interpreting Lacan*, New Haven: Yale University Press, pp. 51-74.

Richardson, William J. (1983b) "Psychoanalysis and the Being Question" in: Joseph H. Smith and William Kerrigan, eds., *Interpreting Lacan*, New Haven: Yale University Press, pp. 139-159.

Richardson, William J. (1983c) « La Psychanalyse et la question de Dieu, » *Foi et raison à partir de Sainte Thomas. Le Discours Psychanalytique*, VIII (September): 17-20. (a more developed version published in English in 1986).

1985

Richardson, William J. (1985) "Lacanian Theory" in: A. Rothstein, ed., *Models of the Mind: Their Relationship to Clinical Work*, New York: International Universities Press, pp. 101-117.

1986

Richardson, William J. (1986) "Psychoanalysis and the God-Question," *Thought*, 61: 68-83.

1986-1987

Richardson, William J. (1986-1987) "Psychoanalysis and Anti-humanism: Lacan's Legacy," *Krisis: Journal for Contemporary Philosophy*, 5: 61-80.

1987

Richardson, William J. (1987a) "Ethics and Desire," *The American Journal of Psychoanalysis*, 47(4): 296-301.

Richardson, William J. (1987b) "Meaning in Psychoanalysis," *Phenomenology—Meaning—Psychotherapy, The Second Annual Symposium of the Simon Silverman Phenomenology Center*, Duquesne University. Pittsburgh: The Simon Silverman Phenomenology Center, pp. 89-107.

Richardson, William J. (1987c) "Contemplative Action," in J.W. Bernauer, ed., *Amor Mundi: Explorations in the Faith and Thought of Hannah Arendt*, Dordrecht (Netherlands): Nijhoff Publishers, pp. 115-133.

Richardson, William J. & Muller, John P (1987) *Ouvrir les Écrits de Lacan*, adapte par P. Julien. Toulouse: Erès. Reprinted in 1993.

1988

Richardson, William J. (1988a) "Lacan and the Problem of Psychosis," in: David Allison, Nyth. de Olivera, Mark Roberts and Allen Weiss, eds., *Psychosis and Sexual Identity: Towards a Post-modern View of the Schreber Case*, Albany: SUNY Press, pp. 18-29.

Richardson, William J. (1988b) "Lacan and Non-Philosophy" in: Hugh J, Silverman, ed., *Philosophy and Non-Philosophv since Merleau-Ponty*, New York: Routledge, pp. 120-134.

Richardson, William J. (1988c) "The Subject of Hermeneutics and the Hermeneutics of the Subject," in: *Hermeneutics and the Tradition, Proceedings of the American Catholic Philosophical Association*, LXII: 29-45, reprinted in *Graduate School Journal* (New School for Social Research – 1990)

Richardson, William J. and John P. Muller, Editors (1988a) *The Purloined Poe: Lacan, Derrida, and Psychoanalytic Reading*. Baltimore: The John Hopkins University Press.

Richardson, William J. and John P. Muller (1988b) "The Challenge of Deconstruction" in: Muller and Richardson, eds., *The Purloined Poe: Lacan, Derrida, and Psychoanalytic Reading*, Baltimore: The John Hopkins University Press. Pp. 159-172.

1989

Richardson, William J. (1989a) "Golden Cup and Silver Bag: On the Catholic University," *America* (November 11): 315-318.

Richardson, William J. (1989b) "Review of M.G. Thompson's *Death and Desire: A Study in Psychopathology*. New York: New York University Press," *Theoretical and Philosophical Psychology*, 9(2): 54-58.

Richardson, William J. and J. Clavreul (1989) "The Stakes of Psychoanalysis: An Ethics of the Subject," *Psychoanalysis and Contemporary Thought*, 12: 663-686.

1990

Richardson, William J. (1990a) "Heidegger's Concept of 'World'," in: P. Williams and J. Falconer, eds., *econsidering Psychology: Perspectives from Continental Philosophy*, Pittsburgh: Duquesne University Press, pp. 198-209.

Richardson, William J. (1990b) "Coufontaine Adsum," *Psychoanalysis and Religion*, Baltimore: John Hopkins University Press, pp. 60-73.

1991

Richardson, William J. (1991a) « La vérité dans la psychanalyse » in : *Lacan avec les philosophes*. Paris: Albin Michel, pp. 191-200.

Richardson, William J. (1991b) "Review of E. Roudinesco's *Lacan & Company: A History of Psychoanalysis in France, 1925-1985*. Chicago: Chicago University Press," *America* (June 15): 657-659.

Richardson, William J. (1991c) "Law and Right," *Cardoza Law Review*, XIII: 1339-1342.

Richardson, William J. (1991d) "On Teaching Epictetus" in: M. Collins and F. Ambrosio, eds., *Text and Teaching. The Search for Human Excellence*, Washington, DC: Georgetown University Press, pp. 45-50.

1992

Richardson, William J. (1992a) "Love and the Beginning: Psychoanalysis and Religion," *Contemporary Psychoanalysis*, 28: 423-441.

Richardson, William J. (1992b) "Como escribir el nombre de Marilyn Monroe," in: *Lacan en Estados Unidos*, edited and translated by D. Bentolila-Lopez, Rosario (Argentina): *Homo Sapiens*, pages 67-86 (original English text published in 2011)

Richardson, William J. (1992c) "'Like Straw': Religion and Psychoanalysis," in: Paul van Tongeren, et al., eds., *Eros and Eris: Contributions to a Hermeneutical Phenomenology: Liber Amicorum for Adriaan Peperzak*. Dordrecht: Kluwer Academic Publishers, pp. 93-104. (A French translation was published in 1994 "Comme de la paille," in *Ibn Rochd [Averroès], Maïmonide, Saint Thomas, ou La filiation entre foi et raison*. Le Colloque de Cordoue, Paris: Climats, Association Freudienne International, pp. 183-201.)

Richardson, William J. (1992d) "The Third Generation of Desire," *The Letter*, Vol. 1: 1117-1135; reprinted in: François Raffoul and David Pettigrew, eds., *Disseminating Lacan*, Albany: State University of New York Press, 1996, pp. 171-188.

Richardson, William J. (1992e) "Desire and its Vicissitudes," in *Phenomenology and Lacanian*

Psychoanalysis: The Eight Annual Symposium of the Simon Silverman Phenomenology Center (Duquesne University), published by the Simon Silverman Center, Pittsburgh, Pa., pp. 13-36.

Richardson, William J. (1992f) "Heidegger's Truth and Politics" in: Arleen Dallery and Charles Scott with Holly Roberts, eds., *Ethics and Danger: Essays on Heidegger and Continental Thought*, Albany: State University of New York Press, pp. 11-24.

1993

Richardson, William J. (1993a) "Dasein and the Ground of Negativity: A Note on the Fourth Movement in the Beiträge-Symphony," *Heidegger Studies*, Vol. 9: 35-52.

Richardson, William J (1993b) "Review of J.-Luc Marion's *God Beyond Being*, Chicago: Chicago University Press (1991)," *Theological Studies*, Vol. 54: 576-578.

Richardson, William J. (1993c) "Heidegger among the Doctors" in: John Sallis, ed., *Reading Heidegger: Commemorations*, Bloomington: Indiana University Press, pp. 49-63.

1994

Richardson, William J. (1994a) "Lacan and the Enlightenment: Antigone's Choice," *Research in Phenomenology*, Vol. 24: 25-41.

Richardson, William J. (1994b) "Preface to P Julien's *Jacques Lacan's Return to Freud*. New York: New York University Press, pages xv-xviii

Richardson, William J. (1994c) "The Word of Silence" in: S. Shamdasani and M Mÿuunchow, eds., *Speculations after Freud. Psychoanalysis, Philosophy and Culture*, London: Routledge, pp. 167-184.

Richardson, William J. (1994d) "Veritá e Politica in Heidegger," G. Colombini, trans., *Humanitas: Rivista Bimestrale di Cultura* (Brescia), No. 6: 796-813.

1995

Richardson, William J. (1995a) "The Irresponsible Subject" in: Adriaan Peperzak, ed., *Ethics as First Philosophy, The Significance of Emmanuel Levinas for Philosophy, Literature and Religion*, New York: Routledge, pp. 123-131.

Richardson, William J. (1995b) "Martin Heidegger" in: Babette Babich, ed., *From Phenomenology to Thought, Errancy and Desire. Essays in Honor of William J. Richardson S.J.*, Dordrecht: Kluwer, pp. 619-629; also published in D. Borchert, ed., *Encyclopedia of Philosophy Supplement*, New York: Macmillan (1996), pp. 233-340.

Richardson, William J. (1995c) "Heidegger's Fall," *American Catholic Philosophical Quarterly*, LXIX: 229-253; reprinted in B. Babich, ed., *From Phenomenology to Thought: Essays in Honor of William J. Richardson S.J.*, Dordrecht: Kluwer Academic Publishers (1995), pp. 619-629.

Richardson, William J. (1995d) "Review of *Paul Ricoeur*, by O Mongin. Paris: Editions du Seuil," *Philosophy and Social Criticism*, Vol. 21: 205-207.

Richardson, William J. (1995e) "An Unpurloined Autobiography" in: James R. Watson, ed., *Portraits of American Continental Philosophers*, including photographs by the editor. Bloomington (Indiana): Indiana University Press, pp. 145-152.

1997

Richardson, William J. (1997a) "Long Day's Journey into Sublimation," *Journal of the British Society for Phenomenology*, vol. 28: 63-79.

Richardson, William J. (1997b) "Review of E Roudinesco's *Jacques Lacan*, translated by Barbara Bray. New York: Columbia University Press (1997)," *America*, CXVII (issue of November 29); reprinted in *Journal of the American Psychoanalytic Association*, (2000), 48: 644-647.

Richardson, William J. (1997c) "From Phenomenology through Thought to a Festschrift," *Heidegger Studies*, Vol. 13: 17-28.

1998

Richardson, William J. (1998a) "Lacan" in: Simon Critchley and William R. Schroeder, eds., *A Companion to Continental Philosophy* (Blackwell Companion to Philosophy), Oxford: Blackwell, pages 519-529

Richardson, William J. (1998b) "In the Name of the Father: the Moral Law?" in Richard Kearney and M Dooley, eds., *Questioning Ethics: Contemporary Debates in Philosophy*, London: Routledge, pp. 201-219.

1999

Richardson, William J. (1999a) "Back to the Future?" in: Frank Ambrosio, ed., *The Question of Christian Philosophy Today*, New York: Fordham University Press, pp. 3-36.

Richardson, William J. (1999b) "The Subject of Ethics," *The Psychoanalytic Review*, 86: 547-567.

2001

Richardson, William J. (2001) "Psychoanalytic Praxis and the Truth of Pain" in: Babette Babich, ed., *Philosophy of Science, Van Gogh's Eyes, and God: Hermeneutic Essays in Honor of Patrick A. Heelan, S.J..* Dordrecht (Netherlands): Kluwer Academic Publishers, pp. 333-343, republished in François Raffoul and David Pettigrew, eds., *Heidegger and Practical Philosophy*, Albany (NY): SUNY Press (2002), pp. 339-358.

2003

Richardson, William J. (2003a) "Heidegger and Psychoanalysis?," *Natureza Humana*, Vol. 5 (1): 9-38.

Richardson, William J. (2003b) "Truth and Freedom in Psychoanalysis" in Roger Frie, ed., *Understanding Experience: Psychotherapy and Postmodernism*, New York: Routledge, pp. 77-99.

2005

Richardson, William J. (2005a) "Continental Philosophy: Towards the Future?," *Budhi: A Journal of Ideas and Culture*, volume 9(1): 19-27.

Richardson, William J. (2005b) "On Heidegger to Lacan – An Interview with William J Richardson, with the participation of Mario L Beira PhD and Sara E Hassan MD (June 21, 2005; Dublin, Ireland)," *Acheronta*, Vol. 22 (December). Online.

http://www.acheronta.org/reportajes/richardson-en.htm.

2009

Richardson, William J (2009) "Waiting for Godot," lecture presented at the annual meeting of the Society for Phenomenology and Existential Philosophy (31 October 2009, Fordham University, Sheraton: New York); Video recording by Babette Babich, available via Fordham University Library Video on Demand http://digital.library.fordham.edu/cdm/singleitem/collection/BabBabich/id/28/rec/28 also in segments, https://www.youtube.com/watch?v=NwTKECXOwiE Online. [Ken Liebermann also recorded this lecture — from a better vantage point with a better camera — but this recording has not been made available (as yet).]

2010

Richardson, William J (2010a) "Foreword" to Richard Capobianco's *Engaging Heidegger*. Toronto (Canada): University of Toronto Press, pp. ix-xv.

Richardson, William J. (2010b) "Towards an Ontology of Bob Dylan [text of a lecture delivered in 1966]," *Philosophy and Social Criticism*, 36 (7): 763-774.

Richardson, William J. (2010c) « Heidegger et la psychanalyse » in : *Penser la clinique psychanalytique*, sous la direction de Gilles Chagnon, Marie Hazan et Michel Peterson. Montreal: Liber; pp. 197-220.

2011

Richardson, William J. (2011) "Philosophy and Psychoanalysis: The Spelling of Marilyn Monroe" (a lecture in honor of Thomas Blakely – March 29, 1990), *The Letter: Irish Journal of Lacanian Psychoanalysis* (Autumn Issue), pp. 9-30.

Richardson, William J., with numerous friends and colleagues (2011) Video: *The Passion of Thought: An Intellectual Biography of Dr. William J. Richardson, SJ.* Documentary on William Richardson, Video and interviews filmed and produced by Edward McGushin,

Paul Bruno, and Scott Campbell. First screened at the Society for Phenomenology and Existential Philosophy in Philadelphia, October 2011.

Richardson, William J., with Babette Babich (2011) Video: *William J. Richardson on Heidegger's Being and Time (with reflections on Errancy and Truth)*. Interview, in one question, filmed at St Mary's, Boston College, using only natural light, at the end of day. Prepared in response to Bill's expressed lack of opportunity to speak in the above noted documentary of his life. Videography: Babette Babich.

Online.
https://www.youtube.com/watch?v=ab7XkaC6LVU

Bill Richardson, Boston College, 8 October 2011

Acknowledgments

Reflections of the various kinds offered here are expressions of gratitude. And the volume as such is likewise a gift. I am grateful to everyone who contributed, most especially, Leo O'Donovan, S.J..

I thank Tracy Burr Strong for helping proofread at least one of the several versions but also for driving with Bill Richardson and myself from Zurich to Meßkirch in May, 2015 and helping me to assist Bill just as intrusively as needed — sometimes this, too, is positive *Fürsorge* — permitting Bill's full participation, just as if no assistance had been given.

And, long ago now, I thank Holger Schmid for driving with Bill and myself to Todtnauberg, Meßkirch, various sites on the Bodensee, and to Italy.

Photographs are mine unless otherwise indicated.

www.ingramcontent.com/pod-product-compliance
Lightning Source LLC
Chambersburg PA
CBHW060030180426
43196CB00044B/2357